CONNOR COURT QUARTERLY

Number 7, Winter 2013

Contents

CONNOR COURT QUARTERLY

ISSN 1839-0129 (Print)
ISSN 1839-0137 (Online)
ISBN (Numbers 7) 9781922168719

Published by Connor Court Publishing Pty Ltd
PO Box 224W, BALLARAT, 3350, www.connorcourt.com

© Connor Court Publishing Pty Ltd

Printed in Australia, Cover design by Ian James

Contacts: Editor- Brian Coman, brian@connorcourt.com;
Sales: sales@connorcourt.com; advertising: anthony@connorcourt.com

Editorial Team

Dr. Brian Coman (Editor) initially trained as a research scientist in the biological sciences but upon retirement returned to the Academy and gained a PhD in the humanities. He writes frequently for *Quadrant* and has published two books as well as many scientific papers.

Maurice Nestor is Assistant Editor and Literary Editor of Connor Court Quarterly. He was for many years a senior lecturer in humanities. He has taught literature and the history of art, mostly in Australia, more briefly in the United States. He has had sketches and travel articles published in *Quadrant*, *Australian Short Stories*, and the Melbourne *Age*. Most recently, he has written on Augustine's *Confessions*, and on the poetry of Andrew Marvell

Dr. Roger Sworder started Latin at six and Greek at ten in English private schools. He has degrees from Oxford and the ANU and lectured in Bendigo for thirty six years. His major studies are on Homer, Parmenides and Plato, and on the theory of work. He is about to publish his third book, a book of essays, in America. He believes that religious differences are much less important now than the difference between the religious in general and the aggressively secular.

Submission Guidelines

Connor Court Quarterly welcomes contributions from readers. Submitted work must address the broad themes as outlined in our mission statement. Contributions should be aimed at the non-specialist, but reasonably well-informed lay reader. There should be a minimum of jargon and highly technical words. Contributions may consist of longer, formal essays or shorter, non-referenced pieces (see below).

All manuscripts should be submitted in electronic form, preferably in MS Word. Shorter contributions may be typewritten and submitted as hard copy, provided they can be easily scanned and converted to electronic copy.

Minimum line spacing is 1.5, using a popular and easily legible typeface, preferably Times New Roman. Suggested lengths for various article types are as follows:

* Short Commentary/Reflections, not referenced (magazine section, see below) 1000-1500 words
* Formal Essays with somewhat wider scope, referenced 3000-5000 words
* Review articles with sub-headings and references 6000-10,000 words
* An opportunity will also exist for the publication of short, original poems.

Each author must include a short biography of no more than 150 words, detailing background and qualifications. All submitted work must be carefully checked and proofed before being offered. References should be indicated in the text with superscript numbers which refer to the source document details arranged as footnotes. Refer to current issue for style. A variable percentage of all published work will be from invited authors

Letters to the Editor will be considered for publication. Preference will be given to shorter letters addressing issues aired in previous issues of the journal. Letters must include name, postal address and email address of sender.

Opportunity for wider reader involvement will also be given in the 'magazine' section of CCQ. Here readers are invited to submit short articles/reflections, poems, and book reviews. References and contributor's biography are not required. Articles and book reviews in this section of CCQ should be brief (<1500 words). The amount of poetry to be published will be very limited and all submitted poems must not exceed a single page of the magazine.

There will be no payments to authors for publication of hard copies of essays, etc., but material accessed online by readers will attract a royalty payment of 10% of the publisher's receipts.

Editor: Brian Coman
brian@connorcourt.com

About This Publication

Connor Court Quarterly (CCQ) is a periodical, non-subscription magazine whose focus is on the history, culture and religion in the Western Tradition. By the term *Western Tradition*, we mean that distinctive mix of languages, formal institutions (especially universities), cultural practices and achievements, and philosophical and religious outlooks which had their genesis in ancient Greece and Rome, their gradual development in the history of Europe, and their subsequent transmission to the New World after the Age of Discovery.

We believe that the achievements of this Tradition are now under attack from many quarters with negative implications for the maintenance of a common moral order, for a shared understanding of what it means to be human, and for a similar shared understanding of the limitations of human achievement. The magazine hopes to be a vehicle for the transmission of those areas of culture which have enriched the Western mind since the time of Homer.

Whilst this may be interpreted as a broadly conservative outlook, the editorial board of CCQ believes that the focus of this new magazine sets it apart from what might be termed 'standard' conservatism. Today, a great deal of what passes for conservative thought is actually a species of liberalism. It has its genesis in the European Enlightenment and is generally dismissive of that whole period between the fall of the Roman Empire and the Reformation. Popular conservatism is also often aggressively secular in outlook and, while it may pay lip service to religious belief, it often sees religion as obscurantist. For CCQ, the term *Tradition* is inescapably linked to religion, making it much more than simply a set of customs or habits. Moreover, it is only within the bounds of an intact Tradition (with its attendant religious beliefs) that *any* moral rules can be validated.

Some Essays in Previous Issues
of Connor Court Quarterly
(available separately)

Issue One - 2011

* Philosophy in a Dark Age – Roger Sworder
* Objectivity: Mathematics and Morals – James Franklin
* Andrew Marvell: Poetry in a Time of War – Maurice Nestor
* A Man for All Seasons: Illegitimacy, Race and the Strange Passions of Albert Leffingwell – Philippa Martyr
* Stewardship: A Foundation for Catholic Reflection on Questions of the Environment – Bishop Julian Porteous

Issue Two – 2011

* Saint Thomas More's Conscientious Objection – Mishka Gora
* The Classical Tradition – Greg Melleuish
* Exclusionists and Confusionists – Michael Connor
* Puritanism and the Origins of Modern Science in the West – Brian J. Coman
* Aspects of the British Riots – Hal G. P. Colebatch

Issue Three – 2012

* Reflections on Secularisation – Greg Melleuish
* Thinking about "Tradition": A Perennialist Perspective – Harry Oldmeadow
* Gawain, the Green Knight and the Proving of Virtue – Maurice Nestor
* From Aesop to Orwell: The Roots of Doubletalk – Stewart Justman

Issue Four – 2012

* Henry Adams and Notre Dame Cathedral at Chartres – John Nethercote
* 'Render Therefore Unto Caesar …'– Roger Sworder
* Evangelism, the British Empire and its Aborigines – Gregory Haines
* William Blake and the Perversion of Pity – Dorothy Avery
* Kipling, Betjeman and the World's Width – Hal G.P. Colebatch

Order your issue online – www.connorcourt.com

$14.95 a copy, $9.95 for the electronic version.

Editorial

The recent election of a new Pontiff in the Catholic Church has occasioned much media comment, not the least of which has been a renewal of the debate over the Church's response to modernity. Is it the role of the Church to seek to accommodate the demands of the age or, rather, is it to seek those changes in modernity which would better suit its Tradition and its doctrines? This is, more than anything else, a question of where adaptation ends and spiritual degeneration begins. This, in turn, raises questions concerning the hierarchy of spiritual goods and the interpretation of the word "tradition" as it applies to Catholicism. In this issue of *Connor Court Quarterly*, two important and passionate essays, the first by Elena Pasquini Douglas and the second by Philippa Martyr, take opposing views on the response of the Church to modernity. A third essay by Rod Blackhirst, a non-Catholic academic, suggests that perhaps Catholics are unduly concerned about the general problem of Modernism as it relates to the Church.

In order to clarify the issues here and to provide some very necessary background, this whole question must be seen in the light of Western history since the Enlightenment, especially the history of philosophy and of those institutions charged with the responsibility of teaching that discipline. In this regard, the essay by Roger Sworder on militant empiricism and the universities is especially important. Whilst most readers of *Connor Court Quarterly* are well aware of the general malaise now deeply embedded in our universities, few have been able to perceive, as Sworder has, its root cause. Sworder, who is also outside the Catholic tradition, sees the poets as presenting the clearest vision of the great war between two competing belief systems – that of traditional religious belief and that of the new secular empiricism, so closely identified with the Anglosphere. This essay actually complements his review of a new publication on the universities (*On the Purpose of a University Education*) also contained in this issue.

In keeping with the general aim of CCQ to promote the great literature and art of the Western Tradition, this issue also contains an essay on the 17th C 'metaphysical' poet, Henry Vaughan, by the Editor, and another essay, by Maurice Nestor, on the great dome of Santa Maria del Fiore in Florence, designed by Brunelleschi. Both, in their own way, relate back to the main theme of this issue. Vaughan's poetic output was hugely influenced by the destructive force of Cromwell's purge of the Anglican Church. His response was to write poetry which looked back towards the Middle Ages and to a religious appreciation of the natural world where nature was not merely a spectacle or mechanism but was, in some sense, sacramental. In this, he ideally fits Sworder's mould of the poet both as conserver and as prophet. With Brunelleschi, we have yet another facet of the story. The builders of the great Medieval cathedrals remained anonymous, believing themselves to be mere instruments of the Almighty. But, as Nestor ably shows, when Vasari published the first edition of his famous *Lives of the Artists* in 1550, Brunelleschi had become the very type of the new Artist, hugely conscious of his own abilities and very much the self-made man. Here again is another marker along the way from man as humble and obedient servant to man as the measure of things. It highlights yet again that insistent question: where does human reason end and Faith begin? That, after all, is the nub of things.

Brian Coman

LETTER TO A NEW WORLD POPE 1[1]

The Catholic Church and the Republic of Modernity

Elena Pasquini Douglas

"Francis, don't you see that my house is being destroyed?" Francis of Assisi heard Christ call, "Go and rebuild my Church".[2] As scandal and avarice eroded the Church from within, and heresies flourished without, Francis led a reform movement by his example of simplicity, humility and virtue. Jorge Mario Bergoglio's decision to take the name of the world's most popular saint was a stroke of genius. This man who catches buses, cooks his own meals and has renounced the princely accoutrements of the Church has endeared himself to the world. On Easter Thursday he added another layer to the story when he washed the feet of young Muslim prisoners, male and female, in an act of tenderness which captured the world's imagination. The Church hasn't had such positive headlines in a decade.

While the honeymoon may soon be over – the world's press will drill into the complexity of his role in Argentina during its darkest years – an afterglow is likely to remain, and continue to be rekindled by this man's extraordinary,

---

[1] This article first appeared in electronic form at http://www.abc.net.au/religion/articles/2013/04/08/3732311.htm

[2] Delio et al. *"Go, Rebuild My House", Franciscans and the Church Today*. Tradepaper Publishers, 2004.

natural acts of genuine charity and compassion. He has a certain pastoral genius. His efforts at deep reform, however, face myriad challenges.

Benedict's brave decision to change the balance of powers between heaven and earth declared the future no country for old men. It seemed a declaration that the time for a new engagement with the modern world had arrived. Although Francis looks likely to maintain doctrinal fidelity, structurally he walks and talks like a reformer. Together, these events suggest that a new age in the Church is dawning.

To modern eyes, the Church looks weak and ailing, plagued by scandal and challenged by charges of irrelevance to the modern world. The crisis of confidence is, of course, understandable given the many failings of the Church in its long history. The sins are real. The sex abuse crisis, along with the Church leadership's failure to respond with compassion and justice, will stain the Church for decades. The painful process of redemption is still in its infancy, but the Church has ridden times of far greater crisis and endured. From Francis' comments, he seems to understand that to do its work, the Church must dwell in the modern imagination. The Church and the Republic of Modernity speak different languages, and privilege different virtues. The Church values continuity and endurance, while modernity praises novelty and efficiency. Dialogue between people with different worldviews, like learning another language, takes discipline and practice. The Church's job is to translate Christ's wisdom into the language, and the worldview, of the day. Without this, Christ's message that "love heals" can simply not be shared. In this task, the Church is failing. Too often it allows its antipathy toward modernity to shine stronger than its love for humanity. In this way, it denies itself crucial knowledge necessary to advance its mission. Catholicism betrays itself and its message by becoming a separated ghetto of nostalgic piety.

This article is about all that is lost in translation between the Catholic Church and the Republic of Modernity. It is an attempt to ask what would be gained if Francis were able to lead the Church, to bend the Curia and the world's dioceses, into an honest and meaningful engagement with the modern world; a return to the ideals of St Francis, as much as those of Vatican II.

To see the Church through modern eyes is to miss her beauty. Many moderns, of course, would like to see the Church turn to dust; others doubt she can survive. They question both her capacity and purpose in the modern world. Her forms, imagination, centralisation, and exclusion all seem anathema to the standards of the modern-scientific age. The many stains on her history are well-known. Catholic Church-bashing is almost a modern sport of the new atheists: a new colosseum, with a new generation of Christians fed to the lions of public opinion.

But this cuts both ways. The Church has a clear eye on modernity's limits. From the Church's vantage-point, the fatal conceit of modernity is that it thinks it has reached the promised land, the end of history, by means of science itself. But science reduces the world into visible or measurable cause-and-effect. Science focuses on each part in ever-greater clarity, but is no grand-master when it comes to the sweeping narrative of life.

3

The pillars of modernity – democracy, science, economics and the self – are means of achieving other ends. The modern-scientific world-view yields a two-dimensional picture, silent on the third dimension: that of meaning and purpose. This renders modernity constitutionally blind to the power of an institution which concerns itself (at its best) with bringing Christ's wisdom and love to life. Reason untempered by faith is thus as dangerous as faith untempered by reason (precisely the point of Benedict's Regensburg lecture).[3] Modernity may be a biased critic, but engagement between the two worlds should still yield fruit. Leaps of human creativity have always come from exchange between profoundly different worlds. The Mughal Empire (the meeting of the Muslim and Hindu worlds), the Renaissance (the wisdom of the Classical age and the structured medieval mind) are but two examples from many.

Contained herein are some impressionistic suggestions and some questions for Pope Francis to consider; an early map of the possible terrain. The first of these is the question of what is at risk if the Church fails to hand on its gifts to future generations. My second intention is to suggest some ideas on structural change, to enable the Church to progress by re-embracing what it has long preached: subsidiarity. My third intention is to revisit the parable of the talents for the modern world: specifically, how the Church can replenish its supply of talent, and therefore knowledge, and bring new abilities and perspectives to the table.

---

[3] Schall, V. James, *The Regensberg Lecture,* St. Augustines Press, Indiana, 2007.

Spiritual and artistic treasures

The art and letters, architecture, painting and sculpture that adorn the Christian canon is a sacred treasury which risks being inaccessible to the next generation. The Church is also a living museum for the humanities, an ark which houses the wisdom of over four thousand years: from the Egyptian idea of the after-life; to Abraham, Moses and the Jewish Patriarchs; to Plato, Aristotle and the classical world; to the religious symbolism and paraphernalia of the vanquished Etruscans; to the ascetic and monastic wisdom of the Desert Fathers and Benedict; to the power and pageantry of the collective Roman and Byzantine worlds.

And, in every age, the Church has taught the arts of living. As contemporary authors like philosopher Alain de Botton[4], and sociologist Robert Putnam[5] have pointed out, the Church retains knowledge and skill in many of the lost arts of living: building communities, serving the needs of others, living a life of sacred covenants, sacraments and spiritual growth.

The Church offers comfort when modernity's promise of control and order fails. For we humans suffer, are left behind in the race of life, are hurt, fail, find ourselves confused, unable to fathom our inner canyons, or our place in the world. And then finally, we face death. Even the secular philosopher Habermas describes "the awkwardness of non-religious burial practices", and how the "modern age has failed to find a suitable replacement for a religious way of coping with the final rite of

[4] De Botton, A. *Religion for Atheists*, Penguin, 2012.
[5] Putnam, R. *How Religion Divides and Unites Us*, Simon & Schuster, 2012.

passage".[6] Believers, then, will always be strangers in this land, because in the depth of its nature modernity does not have room for the soul.

Beyond individual comfort – the perennial concern of the modern heart – since the time of Jesus, Christians have stood in solidarity with the poor and vulnerable. Compassion has animated many in the Church, for a hundred generations. Today over 50% of all healthcare in Africa is delivered by the Catholic Church, the planet's most widely distributed welfare-network. Will that be sustained by the next generation in the absence of radical reform?

The modern world has largely lost access to the magnificent artistic, practical, intellectual and spiritual endowment that is a gift to humanity. Even Benedict's luminous encyclicals didn't make it beyond the inner-sanctum of conservative churchgoers. Francis must find a way for the gifts of the Church to be shared with the modern world.

The Church's longevity has been understood as flowing from her capacity to reconcile endurance with change and to deal creatively with dissent; a Church that could contain multitudes. In recent times the Church has largely lost this facility. Jaroslav Pelikan proposed that tradition "is the living faith of the dead; traditionalism is the dead faith of the living".[7] Benedict echoed the ideal, but lacked the executive skills or the insight into life. Pope Francis must help the Church to be a learning institution once more.

[6] Habermas J. et al. *An Awareness of What Is Missing* Trans. Ciaran Cronin. Polity, Cambridge, 2010, p 15.

[7] Pelikan, J. Jaroslav, *The Vindication of Tradition*, Yale University Press, 1984, p. 65.

The view that the Church is now weak is not universal. Eminent Vatican watcher George Weigel cites John Paul II as the architect of a renewed drive to challenge modernity on its own terms. His era was a turning-point from the defensive posture of the counter-reformation.[8] While John Paul II made history as a powerful actor in the great modern drama of the Cold War, Weigel's assessment is that a new evangelisation for the twenty-first century is underway. He does not challenge the cost of the centralisation of John Paul II, undismantled by Benedict.

The current top-down Church is not viable in the information age. Subsidiarity, the long-held Church organising principle, that matters ought to be handled by the smallest, lowest, and least centralised competent authority, must be restored by Francis. Subsidiarity resonates with modernity. Modern biology and economics show us that decisions are best made on the ground where they can incorporate local conditions, adaptations and opportunities. Francis' description of himself as coming from the "end of the earth" augers well that the Church will now practice what it has long preached.

In fact, the Catholic Church has a special task to properly reconcile itself with economics. The various Papal encyclicals present a confused and inconsistent curriculum, made worse by the various pronouncements by Diocesan Bishops' councils, framed with little economic understanding at all. This must be remedied. Economics is a dominant language of modernity. The Church can little afford not to speak it. At the heart of the

---

[8] Weigel, G., *Evangelical Catholicism: Deep Reform in the 21st-Century Church*. Basic Books, 2013.

Church's struggle to be relevant in prosperous lands is its inability to be consistent about economics.

It is said that the Church today is held together by old men and sticky-tape. But like all institutions – universities, political parties, professions – the Church faces a 'war for talent'. This will likely become the defining issue in the next age. In a choice-rich world, having sufficient stewards, priests, and lay leaders of ability is tough. There have never been more baptised Catholics alive than there are today – 1.3 billion souls[9] – but as the world gets rich, people lose faith. Without change, the Church's numbers will peak in the coming decades and then suffer precipitous decline. Jorge Bergoglio can see that Catholicism thrives no better in Singapore or Chile than it does in Western Europe. A change of course is needed.

The gap is also widening between the clerical Church and its lay leaders. Too many positions require clerical fulfilment. St Francis was not a priest, he was only a deacon; yet he created a Europe-wide revival in the Church. Will the Pope who has taken his name embrace the role of the laity now as crisis looms? In this light, the question of women's contribution in the Church's leadership and evolution will not go away. Left unaddressed, this issue will remain an agony. Eventually the desperate need for talent will force the Church's hand. Just do it now Francis; save the pain.

The great thinkers in every age stand on the shoulders

---

[9] Weigel, George, 'World religions by the numbers', Catholic Education Resource Center, first published 2002, http://www.catholiceducation.org/articles/facts/fm0010.html. Accessed 3 April, 2013.

of giants and help us see further: "newspapers in one hand, Bibles in the other", the halls of the Vatican ought to throng with the best being thought and said. Pope Francis must enter into modernity's beating heart, both its promise and its limits, deriving the lessons for the work of the Church. Humanity deserves an engaged Catholic Church, shaping the imagination of the future. The great synthesisers of evolutionary biology, psychology, economics, and epistemology are coming to a new humility, and new ideas of human solidarity, morality and the origins of virtue. The Church cannot afford *not* to engage with them.

This is the new ecumenism. Pope Francis I will need to engage with modernity, not in pursuit of the shallow liberalism of permissiveness and identity, but to meet the deepest yearnings of humanity for community, freedom and love. The task is to *repent*, from the Latin *to rethink;* to come at anew; to understand differently. He appears to have the leadership ability that Benedict, for all his subtle thinking, lacked. Francis can call Catholics-in-exile to return to rebuild Christ's Church. The exclusion of women from the halls of creativity and leadership will need to be sacrificed to keep faith with a people who know women hold up half the sky. All are needed to help to translate the Church's message into new idioms and world-views, so that this great tradition – the ark of so much of humanity's story – can be shared with an ever-wider world.

It has in fact been the Church's flexibility which has always underwritten its endurance. Thomas Babington Macaulay saw this, and described it in majestic terms:

No other institution is left standing which carries the mind back to the times when the smoke of sacrifice rose from the Pantheon, and when camelopards and tigers bounded in the Flavian amphitheatre. The proudest royal houses are but of yesterday, when compared with the line of the Supreme Pontiffs. That line we trace back in an unbroken series, from the Pope who crowned Napoleon in the nineteenth century to the Pope who crowned Pepin in the eighth; and far beyond the time of Pepin the august dynasty extends, till it is lost in the twilight of fable.

The republic of Venice came next in antiquity. But the republic of Venice was modern when compared with the Papacy; and the republic of Venice is gone, and the Papacy remains. The Papacy remains, not in decay, not a mere antique, but full of life and youthful vigour. The Catholic Church is still sending forth to the farthest ends of the world missionaries as zealous as those who landed in Kent with Augustin, and still confronting hostile kings with the same spirit with which she confronted Attila. The number of her children is greater than in any former age. Her acquisitions in the New World have more than compensated for what she has lost in the Old. ... Nor do we see any sign which indicates that the term of her long dominion is approaching. She saw the commencement of all the governments and of all the ecclesiastical establishments that now exist in the world; and we feel no assurance that she is not destined to see the end of them all. She was great and respected before the Saxon had set foot on Britain, before the Frank had passed the Rhine,

> when Grecian eloquence still flourished at Antioch,
> when idols were still worshipped in the temple of
> Mecca. And she may still exist in undiminished
> vigour when some traveller from New Zealand
> shall, in the midst of a vast solitude, take his stand
> on a broken arch of London Bridge to sketch the
> ruins of St. Paul's.[10]

Macaulay's account for her success is that she could be a Church which could deal with different enthusiasms and responses; a church which contained multitudes.

Pope Francis inherits the responsibility to make the changes that will prevent the Church – and her spiritual, intellectual and artistic treasures – being "lost in the twilight of fable". [11] To do this he will need to bring the two worlds together – the Catholic Church and the Republic of Modernity – to break bread. Perhaps then they can create a new synthesis of truth, beauty and goodness. The poet Arthur O'Shaughnessy whispered that "each age is a dream that is dying, or one that is coming to birth".[12] May the prayer in the heart of this first new world Pope be not for fidelity to the dream that is dying, but to the one that, with the help of the right midwives, he could bring to birth.

---

[10] Macaulay, Thomas Babington. "Von Ranke." In: *Critical and Historical Essays*, vol. 3. Longman, Brown, Green and Longmans, 1848. http://www.gutenberg.org/ebooks/28046. Accessed 4 April 2013.

[11] Ibid.

[12] O'Shaughnessy, Arthur. 'Ode', (Louis Untermeyer, ed), *Modern British Poetry,* 1920. http://www.bartleby.com/103/6.html (accessed 3 April, 2013).

****

*Elena Pasquini Douglas is the Convenor of the Centre
for Social Impact at the University of Western Australia
Business School. She is completing a PhD in Virtue and
Economics and writes regularly as a social and economic
policy commentator for the* Australian Financial Review

LETTER TO A NEW WORLD POPE II
The Roman Catholic Church and the Republic of Modernity

Philippa Martyr

I never thought I'd find myself writing a set of suggestions for a new Pope. This is for several reasons, chiefly that my name is neither Josef Ratzinger nor Phillip Adams. Also I think the Pope is probably pretty busy right now, and in any case if he wanted to know my opinion on anything he could read my blog, or just call me some time (you can find me quite easily via Google). But here goes.

With every new Pontiff, the Republic of Modernity goes mad, which is only to be expected, as its inhabitants do not see anything beyond surface impressions. A new Pope must therefore mean new things – new and shiny things for a new and shiny era, which is over before it even begins. For this we have to thank the very Modern 24-hour news cycle (and as newspapers evaporate like smoke into the electronic era, calls to have them taken seriously as 'modern' sources of information simply show how transient the Modern really is).

The Catholic Church was founded for one reason: to save human beings, body and soul. Its primary mission in time and eternity is not to put food on the table, give people jobs, collect artwork, preserve the intellectual heritage of humanity, or write good music. It's to save souls. All the art-collecting, heritage-preserving, meaningful dialogue and musical composition doesn't matter a damn if it doesn't turn people's minds and hearts back to the God who loves them, and who created them and everything else out of nothing. And it doesn't matter really whether the Catholic Church is led by Benedict III, Pius II or Francis I, because ultimately it is led by Christ Jesus, and His mandate never changes.

The current top-down Church is actually the same top-down Church that was founded by Jesus when He gave the keys to Peter. Even the most casual reading of the Acts of the Apostles reveals a top-down Church in operation, and an eminently viable one, even in that 'non-information age'. In fact, given the brevity of our current 'information age', I would be asking questions about *its* viability rather than that of a tried-and-tested 2000 year old institution.

The Catholic Church exists to relieve people – individual people, which would be you and I and everyone else – from the misery of fallen human existence, and to draw them up into Heaven when they die. Every person on earth is trapped both in their own personal sin and in a society which is fundamentally damaged. Only God has the keys to the door of this mess, and he gave those keys to Peter.

This isn't to say that life on earth doesn't have its moments. But the ceiling of the Sistine Chapel and the Book of Kells and the Ten Commandments and the *Mass in B Minor* are not ends in themselves. They are all tools in a training ground for an eternal life of perfect fulfilment in love. That's the whole purpose of human life – to know that God exists, to know that He loves you, to know that you can love Him back, and that doing so will bring you joy in this life, and perfect joy once this training ground phase is over.

There is no Republic of Modernity. I wish there were, because I'd be out the front of its embassy throwing rocks in solidarity with those who have perished at this Republic's hands – the butchered innocents of the atheistic French Revolution, the slaves plundered from the African coasts to farm the very modern Americas, the starved peoples of 1930s Ukraine, the victims of the gas chambers and gulags across Europe, the millions of Chinese massacred precisely so their country could become thoroughly 'modern'.

No, the Republic of Modernity has no embassy, and no single ambassador, and no one language. Instead, its envoys are legion, its dialects garbled, and its message confused. And as I stand here on the shoulders of giants, from the elevated height of four thousand years of human theological heritage, I can safely say that where there is legion, garbling and confusion, there is only one source – an ancient source, far older than anything I can think of.

This ancient source's connections with the 'Modern' are rarely explored, but its fingerprints can be clearly seen throughout history. They are all over the ritual sacrifice of children in Carthage and adults in Aztec Mexico. And, in the name of the Modern they are all over the avant-garde culture, the up-to-date theology, and the pressing political crisis. They are all over the rape of Berlin, Baader Meinhof and Shining Path, 'art' like Andres Serrano's *Piss Christ*, and (that most thoroughly Modern of sounds) the vacuum suction of the busy abortion clinic.

Against this vile Republic, I am proud to stand. But

really, the Republic of Modernity is just another word for something that St John called 'the world, the flesh and the devil', and it doesn't change much, for all its Modernity. For example, we have the Republic of Modernity to thank for the crisis in priestly numbers in the pampered West. There is no place in that Republic for a poor, chaste, celibate man who lives only for others, worshipping a God that cannot be seen, and denying himself so that he can bring that God to others.

What the Republic wanted – and got from us; a shameful concession – was a priest who was a 'leader' first and foremost; the centre of attention, the star of the show. But that wasn't the Republic's last territorial demand. From there, the Republic wanted that role to be opened to everyone, male or female. This is again the Modern at its most posturing and facile; its most infantile and demanding.

Is there a crisis in priestly numbers worldwide? No. Is there a crisis in priestly numbers in lazy, affluent dioceses with poor seminary programs and priests who try to make Mass an entertainment rather than the worship of God, and where there is little or no real love of the Mass and the priesthood? Yes, absolutely. The problem here is not the priesthood or its maleness. The problem is us, and our lack of prayer for good priests, and our selfish materialism, and our smaller families, and our unwillingness to be generous with vocations from our own families. All these are the fruits of our recently rather lop-sided engagement with the Republic of Modernity.

Has the Church got a poor track record of engaging with the world, the flesh and the devil? Hardly. The

Church exists in time and space, and can't seal itself off hermetically – or even eremetically – from the world it came to save. But seriously, what on earth has the Republic of Modernity to offer the Church? Modernity's view of Church history and its own history is scarcely objective – for example, most of Western history's great scientists have been believers, compared to the handful who weren't. The Society of Jesus weren't exactly sitting on their hands for the four centuries or so that they were recognised by the world as the Church's crack intellectual troops.

To what does the Church owe its longevity? Certainly not to any capacity to deal creatively with dissent – although sometimes the Church's ways of dealing with dissent have been very creative and also extremely Modern, and have involved a world of pain. (Now there's an example of engagement with the Modern that we don't tend to hear about.) The Church's longevity actually flows from its Divine origin and the promise of Jesus that He would always be there with her. This Church has been expressly designed to contain all the birds of the air that want to shelter in its branches.

How and when the Church handles dissent – which is inevitable – is a matter that will change over time, but dissent will never become 'incorporated' into the Church, nor does it strengthen it. When Catholics dissent from Church teachings, they are not part of some imaginary 'loyal opposition'. They are in fact declaring war on Christ's truth. They are of course free to do this, and equally free to accept the consequence, which is separation from Him.

Should we engage with the Republic of Modernity because of its excellent track record on affirmative action? The Catholic Church was way ahead there as well, given that from its inception it provided women from all walks of life with the only feasible alternative to marriage that most cultures could support. What this has to do with women in the priesthood is precisely nothing: women don't actually hold up half the sky, because gravity does that for us, and even if women held up 95% of the sky it still wouldn't justify them becoming Catholic priests – who are not elected, and therefore do not have to be representative of anything or anyone except Christ in his manhood.

And where is the Republic of Modernity's response to global and individual poverty, sickness, abandonment, rejection and marginalisation? I am still waiting to see Atheists Without Borders doing even a fraction of the good in this world that the Church did in just its first century of existence. You need a burning engine of love to do that kind of work before there are camera crews to record it and people to sing your praises on daytime TV. The Republic has no heart; the Church is nothing but heart.

To over-engage with the Republic of Modernity actually holds the Church back, rather than driving it forward. The Church is the vanguard of humanity, not the guard's van. All previous attempts to over-engage with the 'Modern' in any century have led to the Church being taken prisoner – the Byzantine empire, Gallican France and Reformation England are all very useful examples – and from there it has been persecution, public executions and bad times all round. The most recent example of the

Second Vatican Council has at least not led to public executions.

The Republic of Modernity had a beginning and will have an end: it is a static object hurtling like an arrow in an ever-decreasing trajectory until it loses all its kinetic force, and either impales itself on an obstacle, or falls to the ground useless. The Church also had a beginning, but like a human soul, it is alive: it is a dynamic, living organism that will simply continue throughout time and then throughout eternity. Because it is alive, it is a self-reforming being: it reforms itself constantly to meet the changing needs of the world it came to save. You can watch it like time-lapse photography: religious orders are born, reform and die out, and new ones blossom to take their place, always responding to the needs of the world, but never directed by the world's perceived wants and demands.

He who marries the spirit of the age is a widower in the next, and this has been fulfilled in my own lifetime. I see petrified-in-amber liturgical dinosaurs producing 'Modern' liturgies with 1970s German street theatre production values, which can't hold a candle to the *X Factor* and shouldn't even try. This is of course at the very time that vanguard Catholic churches all over the world are returning to kneeling for Holy Communion, Mass said facing God and facing east, peace, reverence and Gregorian chant. Now *that's* embarrassing.

What the Church does best is save souls. It needs a myriad of ways in which to do this, and it's delightful to see the harnessing of new communication technologies at a cracking pace. But that's not because they are Modern

19

– it's because they work, they're getting cheaper all the time, and they're a good way of reaching people. They can be cast aside very easily for the next thing; and also if we need to return to vellum and quill pens, we've done that before. In other words, the medium is actually not the message.

Is 'Modern' really just a euphemism for 'pagan'? The Church has a long and well-established way of dealing with pagans, and that's to convert them. When I think of that image of the gates of hell not prevailing, I used always think of a pair of gates battering against a rock, but what it's really describing is the Church as a battering ram against the gates of the Republic of Modernity. Stand back, because we are coming to get you, and we will not stop until we have conquered in the name of Christ Jesus.

SOME NOTES ON CONTEMPORARY CATHOLICISM

Rod Blackhirst

(Editor's Note: This article was written prior to the election of the new Pontiff)

Religious affairs in general are poorly covered in the mainstream media, but Catholic affairs especially so. To have any accurate sense of what is happening in the Church today one must read widely beyond the usual media sources. The following are a collection of notes on the state and direction of the Church gleaned from a regular survey of blog sites and a wide array of other sources.

• The papacy of Benedict XVI will generally be seen as ineffectual. A theologian and a philosopher, he has not been good at managing the Vatican. But the abdication of Benedict does not signal a crisis or chaos in the Church as a whole. This should be kept in perspective. There have been administrative and financial difficulties in the Vatican itself, but these are not endemic in the Church as a whole.

• The Church is not "in crisis" as the liberal media like to describe it. There is no sense of crisis in the Church. The Church, in fact, is more directed and consolidated now than she has been at any time for the last fifty years.

• The abdication of Pope Benedict XVI will not

reignite the battle between so-called liberals and so-called conservatives. There is no battle. The conservatives won, long ago. The liberal cause is lost. Its last hopes evaporated during the papacy of John Paul II.

• The conservative project to rein in the excesses of the Second Vatican Council and the exaggerated agenda of Vatican II liberals is now complete. The Church now subscribes to a cautious and conservative reading of Vatican II where modernisation is not at the expense of tradition. Ratzinger, as cardinal and as pope, has worked to create the appropriate intellectual edifice and to hose down the liberals and accommodate the most troublesome of the traditionalists. This has been a long process. It has largely been successful. The Church now has a solid, coherent (non-liberal) position on Vatican II and has neutralized many of her traditionalist critics. The liberals are marginalized and irrelevant.

• The College of Cardinals is testimony to the irrelevance of liberals: it is now replete with conservatives. The chances of the next Pope being a "modernist" and a "liberal" are absolutely zero. Zero. Given the structures of the Church, every foreseeable papacy henceforth will be "conservative." The Church is now irrevocably set upon that path.

• Progressives typically think that "progress" is inevitable. They see liberalisation as the march of history and believe that history is on their side (and that conservatives are "on the wrong side of history"). This mentality has now been dislodged from the Church. There is no "inevitability" mind-set. Instead, there is a long term combative view that eventually liberalism will exhaust itself, that the liberal agenda can be reversed and that the Church will prevail. There is a noticeable mood of resilience, endurance and optimism among Church conservatives nowadays. The era when they were in retreat (and described as dinosaurs) has passed.

• The child sex abuse scandal represents only a temporary setback for the Church in the West. It is widely believed among those who matter in the Church that the cause of the problem was the rampant liberalism and lax discipline that followed Vatican II. The cure for the abusive culture, therefore, is greater priestly discipline and a greater emphasis on the value of celibacy. (People who think the Church will scrap celibacy as a response to the child sex abuse scandals are delusional. That will not happen.)

• The most important event of the last few decades has been the terminal decline (collapse) of Protestantism. The Church is being repositioned in this wider context. It is very significant that in the USA – a nation founded upon Protestantism – the recent Republican candidates for the Presidency were a Mormon and a Catholic. American conservativism – once highly suspicious of Catholicism – is now reconciled to it. In some ways, we are witnessing the close of the Reformation. Protestantism exhausted itself into secular liberal relativism (witness the history of the Netherlands in the 20th C as a paradigmatic case, from ultra-Protestant to ultra-secular in two generations).

• The same observation can be made in Australia. The entire politico-religious landscape has changed. Not that long ago, still within living memory, the Labor Party was aligned with an Irish Catholic working class and the

Liberal Party was the bastion of the white anglo-saxon Protestant establishment. There is now a new polarisation. The Christian presence in the Labor Party has all but collapsed. Atheism is now the natural religious position on the progressive side of politics while the Liberal Party is led by a Catholic – something inconceivable until quite recently.

• A distinct danger facing the contemporary Church, arising out of new political polarisations, is the embrace of right wing political interests whose real agenda is radical free market economics. We saw this in Paul Ryan, Mitt Romney's Catholic running mate, whose policy positions were far more extreme than the cautious social teachings of the Church. Corporate anarchism and economic Darwinism are at odds with the more communitarian, distributist focus of the church, specifically as promulgated by Leo XIII late in the nineteenth century. The Church endorses private property and opposes communism, but scripturally, doctrinally, morally and historically she has a profound quarrel with Mammon.

• Although Catholicism is in decline in Europe and the West, it is booming elsewhere. The Church is generally very healthy in Africa, Asia and Latin America. Seen in its totality, and boasting 1.1 billion members, Catholicism is not in decline: rather it is being globalized and losing its historical Eurocentric focus. This is a strength. While it declines in one place, it can build in another. (This is a strategic luxury that Protestantism has not had).

• Too much is made of the "failure" of Benedict's avowed project to re-evangelize Europe. It is a long term project. Church thinking is that as China, India and Brazil become economic giants, power will shift away from Europe. This is in the Church's favour. The de-Christianizing of Europe, while regrettable, is not calamitous because Europe itself is no longer so important. The global Church will be able to re-evangelize Europe – or what is left of it – from the new centres of power in due course.

• Benedict XVI and other conservatives have made it clear that they are prepared to let the Church shrink in the West, rather than compromise church orthodoxy. Benedict drew a useful parallel with Tibetan Buddhism: dislodged in its homeland but with the treasures of its tradition intact. This is the prevailing mentality in the wider Church now. There is no appetite for capitulation to secular liberal values.

• While vocations (priests) are in short supply in the West, and Church attendance is in decline, the Catholic education system (from primary to tertiary levels) is extremely robust and very successful in most countries. It provides a strong platform from which to rebuild. It is also anticipated that the decline of the welfare state will restore the Church's social mission in the West. In its hospitals, schools and welfare agencies the Church has maintained a platform in Western societies even as official Church attendance dips.

• The deeper background to the decline of Protestantism is the arrival of Islamic populations in the West. The Church is not unduly concerned about the threat of Islam to Christianity; she supposes that Islamic migration will tend to produce a pro-Christian backlash. The Islamic threat is seen as a potential boon for the Church. On the other hand, Church thinking views atheist China as a far greater long term threat to the Church than is militant (or demographic) Islam. The greatest challenge facing the contemporary Church is China.

• The number of Protestants converting to Catholicism continues to grow, vastly outstripping the number of Catholics who convert to a Protestant denomination. This has increased in recent decades. American evangelical Protestants made some progress in Latin America in the 1980s-90s, but this has slowed down. (Protestantism is making gains in China because the relatively cumbersome formal structures of Catholicism are more easily obstructed by the Chinese authorities.)

• An increasing number of churches are seeking shelter in the Church of Rome. As Christianity retreats from aggressive secularism, small denominations which might have been previously anti-Catholic are seeking cordial relations with Rome. The Catholic Church is resuming a leadership role among Christians.

• One of the projects of the so-called conservatives has been the revival of Marian spirituality. Vatican II liberals had shied away from the cult of the Blessed Virgin because they saw it as an obstacle to eucumenicism. After decades of decline, the fullness of a vigorous and unapologetic Marian spirituality has now been restored in Church devotionalism. This is probably the most significant spiritual movement in the contemporary Church.

• While conservatives are not inclined to give way on such popular liberal issues as celibacy, contraception or abortion, there is a widely held view that the Church has been unnecessarily hostile to divorcees. This is the one point of liberalisation with wide support across factions. The Church is likely to be more welcoming to divorcees in future. It is one category of ex-Catholics that the Church believes it can win back.

• None of this is to make light of the challenges faced by the contemporary Church. The Church faces the same tensions and difficulties that accompany an expanded globalism as do other institutions. There is a widening disconnect between Vatican bureaucracy and local parishes, for example, and efforts to reform the Curia and other organs of the Church to meet the new realities of the age have encountered some profound and intractable problems. It is clear that these problems – administrative rather than theological – were outside the expertise of Benedict. Before and after becoming Pope he steered the Church through the ideological crisis that followed Vatican II. His successor will need different skills to tackle a new set of challenges.

On the whole, and looking at the big picture, the future looks very promising for Catholicism. The Church is in much better health than most people might suppose.

****

Dr Blackhirst has taught Philosophy and Religious Studies, and related disciplines, at La Trobe University over the past twenty-three years. Although he attended schools serviced by De la Salle Brothers, his background is Protestant and he is not a Roman Catholic. He offers independent commentary on contemporary and historical religious issues.

ACU

AUSTRALIAN CATHOLIC UNIVERSITY

ppi
public
policy
institute

Leading debate …   *for Australia's future*

---

*"Modern universities are more than just teaching and research institutions –
they have a vital role through independent rigorous analysis to lead debate
on critical issues, to disseminate knowledge, to engage with the public and to
develop practical solutions for our nation's future."*

Professor Greg Craven, Vice Chancellor, Australian Catholic University

---

The Australian Catholic University established the Public Policy Institute (PPI) in Canberra to:

• Conduct research to inform public policy

• Provide critical commentary and analysis on current issues

• Engage the community to access ideas and propose solutions

• Do independent policy consultancies

Visit our website to view our many policy initiatives, commentaries and sponsored seminars
and workshops www.acu.edu.au/ppi

The PPI is led by Professor Scott Prasser and supported by Fr Frank Brennan SJ AO, Professor
in Law, the Hon Dr Gary Johns, Associate Professor in Public Policy, J.R. Nethercote, Adjunct
Professor, visiting researchers, Associate Members, an Advisory Committee chaired by Tony
Harris and an energetic research and administrative team.

For further information
02 6209 1248/9

Email: **publicpolicyinstitute@acu.edu.au**

HOW POETS BECAME THE ONLY
PHILOSOPHERS

Roger Sworder

There is a harsh story to tell about the last three centuries of the liberal arts in the Anglosphere. In 1741 at the end of the *Dunciad*, Alexander Pope wrote:

> *Philosophy,* that leaned on Heaven before,
>
> Shrinks to her second cause, and is no more.
>
> *Physic* of *Metaphysic* begs defence,
>
> And *Metaphysic* calls for aid on *Sense!* [1]

Philosophy's second cause here is mechanical causation, as we find for example in Newton's account of gravity in the *Principia Mathematica*. Primary causes are the reasons why the world as it is is best as it is, the operations of divine wisdom in the creation and providential ordering of the world. The distinction is Plato's who supposed that the primary cause of sight in the human being is to enable the seeing of the stars, which will lead to the discovery of number which in turn leads to philosophy. And philosophy is the greatest of all the goods the Gods have given us. Plato explains the secondary cause of sight by an anatomy of the eye and how its parts cooperate to produce vision. Pope is claiming that in his time philosophy as a discipline in England had dispensed

---

[1] Alexander Pope, *Selected Poetry and Prose*, Holt, Rinehart & Winston, USA, 1965, p.449.

with the need to provide primary causes and was satisfied with mechanical explanations alone. For Pope this shift means that there is no more philosophy in England. The works of Francis Bacon and John Locke are not, according to the *Dunciad*, philosophy.

The latter two lines from the *Dunciad* make the same point as powerfully. Aristotle gave an account of many of the categories and terms of the natural sciences in his *Physics* but supposed that these foundations required still further examination as theology, and this is the purpose of his *Metaphysics*. So Physics requires Metaphysics to defend it, but in Pope's time there was no longer a metaphysical theology, but empiricism instead, the theory that all we know derives from sense experience and reflection upon it. Locke's laborious arguments to demonstrate the truth of empiricism are all that is left of metaphysics in Pope's time. Locke's arguments are still, I suppose, metaphysical in that they seek to provide the conceptual foundations of the new science, but they are certainly not theological. And for Pope there is something very strange about the new 'metaphysics' because it appeals for justification to sense-experience and so his exclamation mark.

Both Plato and Aristotle were fascinated by mechanical, secondary causes as well as primary ones, and they devoted much of their lives to the study of the natural world at this level. Nonetheless Pope's distinction stands: the difference between philosophy and the new thinking is that the new thinking does not consider primary causes. Put like this, the new thinking is simply a negation of a certain part of philosophy. It is not strictly an alternative or contrary view. And in this at least the proto-romantic

William Blake was at one with Augustan Pope. Blake too supposed the new thinking of the mechanists to be a negation, not a contrary.

Intellectually Blake was a reactionary, while politically he was progressive. And in this he was like Wordsworth, Coleridge and Keats, all of whom appreciated how the new thinking denatured the beauties of the creation by denying or ignoring its relation to the Divine. Coleridge particularly showed how this was so both in his poems and his philosophical essays. But the clearest account of the rift between philosophy and the new thinking from this point of view is given by the German Novalis in his essay of 1791, *Christendom or Europe.*

> The erudite is by instinct the enemy of the clergy according to the old order. The erudite and the clerical classes, once they are separated, must war to the death, for they strive for one and the same position. This separation advanced ever further, and the erudite gained the more ground the more the history of European humanity approached the age of triumphal erudition, whereas knowledge and faith entered into more decisive opposition. It was to faith that people looked to find the cause of the general impasse, and this they hoped to obviate by keen knowledge. Everywhere the sense for the holy suffered from the manifold persecutions of its previous form, its former personality. The end product of the modern manner of thinking was termed "philosophy," and under that head was reckoned everything that was opposed to the old, hence primarily every objection against religion. The initial personal hatred of the Catholic faith

> passed gradually over into hatred of the Bible, of the Christian faith, and finally of religion in general.[2]

This is the battle of which universities have been the battle-ground ever since. Newton showed how the two forces of inertia and gravity were enough to maintain the heavens in their courses. No God seemed to be needed once they were in motion, whatever Newton himself might privately have thought. Darwin achieved the same simplification with the theory of natural selection. The processes described in the first verses of the Bible could have occurred all by themselves. Where Hegel had argued for an ever-increasing self-awareness of the spirit through human history, Marx supposed that material conditions alone determined human development through the class-struggle, and talk of the spirit was at best a sentimental escape. At the end of the century Freud showed how Plato's Eros, that impulse towards the Divine, was nothing more than the most carnal libido in some tortured sublimation. I find it hard not to see all this as a united and systematic attack on Classical and Christian belief in its previous forms as Novalis prophesied. Its purpose is not to explain but to explain away, to forestall any recourse to primary causes.

But primary causes were not yielded up without a struggle. Against the scientistic reading of Newton, Darwin, Marx and Freud, an impressive array of warriors took their stands, as intelligent as their opponents and much more tuneful. The denunciation of the new thinking

[2] Novalis (pseudonym), 'Christendom or Europe', in *Hymns to the Night and Other Selected Writings* (Transl. Charles E. Passage). Liberal Arts Press, NY, 1960.

by Pope and Blake and the high Romantics was carried on as bravely by the poets before and after the turn of the twentieth century, especially from America. At the end of *Clarel* Herman Melville anatomises and debunks the new atheism. He anticipates a refining of the battle-lines I have described until only the Catholic and the atheist remain. We do not think of Melville as a poet but his crabbed tetrameters in *Clarel* are a concatenation of image and oxymoron which is compelling. At the end of *The Man Against the Sky* Edward Arlington Robinson characterises scientism:

> No planetary trap where souls are wrought
> For nothing but the sake of being caught
> And sent again to nothing will attune
> Itself to any key of any reason
> Why man should hunger through another season
> To find out why 'twere better late than soon
> To go away and let the sun and moon
> And all the silly stars illuminate
> A place for creeping things ...[3]

For Melville and Robinson the new way of thinking is despair, and this bleak vision is maintained by Eliot in *The Waste Land* and by Pound. To these four Americans we may add W. B. Yeats, who was a friend of Pound. Yeats too believed that the garden died when Locke fell into his swoon. We may trace a line then from Pope in the middle of the eighteenth century to the middle of the twentieth century. These poets resisted the new Godless order,

---

[3] Edward Arlington Robinson, "The Man Against the Sky", *The Oxford Book of American Verse*, ed. F.O. Matthiessen, OUP, NY, p.504.

denounced it in the roundest terms and appealed again and again to Christian and Classical theology as the way to make sense of ourselves. The Americans drew upon Emerson in the later nineteenth and twentieth centuries as the English Romantics had drawn on Thomas Taylor. But Yeats and the Americans did not share the Romantic belief in political progress. They were reactionaries in politics as well as intellectually. Otherwise Yeats could fairly describe himself and his friends as the last Romantics.

Not only the poets but even some critics in the university came to feel the terrors of modern scientism. F. R. Leavis was an aficionado of Eliot's *The Waste Land* and coined the marvellously barbaric term Technologico-Benthamism to describe the culture's aberration. Jeremy Bentham was an early Utilitarian. But it was primarily from the poets that the resistance came, not from the critics or the Churches, and so Leavis' extraordinary elevation of the literary in English spiritual life. Compare this with C. P. Snow, a University bureaucrat who blandly argued that the only thing needed to heal the division between the Arts and the Sciences was that experts in each should have a sufficient grounding in the other. If both scientists and literati were literate and numerate, all would be well. But the poets' objections to the new thinking were not the result of their having misunderstood it. They understood it very well.

Meanwhile, the new thinking had been as active as the poets. The Classicist Sir James Frazer reinterpreted the cults of the Greeks and Romans, in which Plato, Aristotle and Plotinus had worshipped, alongside the religious practices of simple peoples around the globe. He took them all to be the pitiable superstitions of darkened minds, seeking through magic to gain that control of the natural world which comes only from the new science. Of Frazer Wittgenstein said that he was more savage than most of his savages who were not as far from understanding spiritual matters as an English man of the twentieth century.[4] Nonetheless, the religious life of Classical antiquity became the material of a new discipline, Anthropology or the study of the human, and so with religion in general.

Early in his career Wittgenstein had been a student of Bertrand Russell and Russell was the most explicitly anti-religious and anti-spiritual 'philosopher' since David Hume in the eighteenth century. The difference was that, unlike Hume, Russell was at the very centre of the university for many decades. With him we may rank Sir Alfred Ayer who argued that the only meaningful propositions were either empirically verifiable or tautologous. Since metaphysical statements are neither, all metaphysical statements are meaningless. This was rescinding from primary causes with a vengeance.

Let us imagine an undergraduate philosophy major in the later twentieth or early twenty-first century which begins with the empiricism of Russell and Ayer. These two are easy writers to read and they set out a standard view very common in the Anglosphere. It is a matter of reception. If you know the history of Western philosophy, then Russell and Ayer take their place as radical opponents of almost all of it. But if you are a first year student they must seem to be straightforward exponents of the laws

---

[4] *Bemerkungen über Frazer's The Golden Bough*, ed. Rush Rees, Synthese, Vol. 17, 1967, pp. 233-253.

which determine our experience and understanding. And very dull. Of course a reading of Russell's *History of Western Philosophy* will set the student right, but this is even more risky, to come to that history through the lens of someone opposed to it. Usually, though, the student is not in a position to see the problem, so it is just dull.

And this is where we are now. The new thinking has been the victor and the older tradition has been so far vanquished as largely to have passed from the common understanding. The resistance to it no longer has a bite. Pope and Blake supposed the new thinking to be the old thinking minus primary causes, a negation of the older view simply and not itself a contrary view. If Pope and Blake were right, then the new thinking cannot survive its own victory any more than the mistletoe survives the last remnants of life in the oak. This great battle, too, will pass into the ether with the *homoiousion* and the *filioque* and the liberal arts as presently practised.

The loss of a negation is not much of a loss. If we define the intellect as the organ which apprehends the Absolute, the loss of the liberal arts as they are now may actually increase the intellectual power of the universities. For it has been said that among professional scientists the incidence of religious belief is high. In their working lives their actions may seem to confirm the spiritless understandings which their worship denies, but primary causes in no way displace secondary causes, and the study of secondary causes has always been entirely compatible with a belief in a providential creation. Odd that the Arts faculties should have been so overwhelmed by the new science when the scientists themselves feel no such compulsion. Nothing could make clearer that it is not the science which has driven the new thinking but the opportunity which the science offered to strike a blow against philosophy and theology.

This leaves open the question of whether it is possible to practise any of the natural sciences without explicit reference to primary causes. Individuals may conduct research into secondary causes but is this activity enough by itself to constitute a science? The answer is no and the same answer must be given in the case of Ecology if it lacks this transcendent and metaphysical dimension. The new British and French schools attempted a simplified, empirical foundation for the natural sciences, but this failed as Hume, Kant and the Idealists showed. Nonetheless that empiricism re-emerged unreconstructed with Russell and Ayer who persuaded many others that there is no spiritual sense to be found in the living of a human life, and that meaning is a property exclusive to propositions. But not metaphysical ones. So we need not bother to seek. John Bull, the English squire, is as much of a philosopher as anyone can safely be, as Berkeley and Hume believed. The University and the Academy in the Anglosphere died then.

But this is only part of our problem. For we have not kept our doubts at home. On the contrary, alongside the missionaries, Western Atheism preached abroad. But this is the subject of another discussion. To open that one and conclude my part in this one, here are some lines of Blake who never even went to secondary school:

I turn my eyes to the Schools & Universities of Europe

And there behold the Loom of Locke, whose Woof rages dire,

Wash'd by the Water-wheels of Newton; black the cloth

In heavy wreathes folds over every nation; cruel Works
Of many Wheels I view, wheel without wheel, with cogs tyrannic
Moving by compulsion each other, not as those in Eden, which,
Wheel within Wheel, in freedom revolve in harmony & peace.[5]

---

[5] William Blake, *Jerusalem, The Emanation of the Giant Albion,* (1804-20), First Chapter, Pl.15, lines 14-20.

BRUNELLESCHI'S DOME

Maurice Nestor

Architecture is an art for the ages, even more than
sculpture is; even more than painting. If there is anything
wrong with the look of a building, it will only look worse
with time; more and more irritating. It may even become,
in time, unbearable. Architecture is also essentially a
public art – you may pass the same building every day;
you may not be able to choose *not* to see it. Hence the
close attention that the architects of the past gave to the
proportions of their buildings, to the height and width and
depth of every part, and the relations between them.

   With this in mind, we turn to Florence: from any distant
view of Florence, you can see the great dome of Santa
Maria del Fiore rising above all the other red rooves of the
city, and above all of its remaining towers. It rises clearly
and cleanly, whether seen from the hills immediately to
the south, or from the more distant hills to the north, where
they rise up to the mass of Mount Morello. The dome is
octagonal in shape; yet it presents the same kind of face,
and the same profile, from whichever direction it is seen.
In his treatise *On Painting*, Alberti wrote of it as "set aloft
in the heavens, ample to cover all the peoples of Tuscany
with its shade".[1] It is one of those buildings that locates
you. Even far out in the hills, once you catch sight of it

---

[1] The passage is much quoted. I have taken it from Elizabeth Holt, ed.,
A Documentary History of Art, Vol. 1; Doubleday Anchor, 1947. Leon
Battista's Alberti's treatise, *De Pictura*, was first published in 1435.

you know where the centre is. Giovanni Fanelli, a modern scholar, says that there are villages out in the Tuscan hills that are called "Apparita", or "Apparenza", because from there you can see the dome off in the distance, like an 'apparition.'

As for the dome itself, it is in perfect equipoise. There is nothing about it that you would want to alter; nothing to regret really, not even in its not quite finished state. It neither presses down on its haunches, as some domes do, nor seeks to escape into the sky, as Gothic spires do. It stands equally between heaven and earth. The greatest dome of eastern Christendom, for example, the Hagia Sophia of Constantinople (Instanbul), gives the impression of tremendous weight and mass, supported by the enormous buttressing structures grouped at its base. This is as it needs to be, since the whole city of Constantinople is built on the fault zone between two continental plates, and is subject to earthquakes. Michelangelo's dome over St Peter's Basilica in Rome is unfortunately obscured, so that it appears awkwardly over the top of its main entrance front, the one most often shown in photographs and on television. (The front is *not* by Michelangelo, by the way, but by Carlo Maderno). It is in danger of seeming unconnected to the structure which it ought to complete. When you do get a clear view of it, as from the less frequented farther end of the Basilica, it sits firmly, strongly, over the main structure, a statement of the majesty of the counter-reformation Catholic Church. The dome of Santa Maria del Fiore in Florence is more graceful, more elastic, its eight faces marked off by the great white ribs that curve upwards and inwards to its crowning lantern, high above the streets of Florence, some 380 feet in the air. It is still the largest masonry dome in the world.[2]

I say that the dome is crowned by this lantern because it can indeed suggest a crown – though that it may do so seems little remarked upon. The eight great white ribs of the dome are completed, and the whole structure locked in place, by the lantern. The line of these ribs is carried up through the buttresses of the lantern in a quickening rhythm to the very top: an elongated cone completed by a golden orb, and surmounted by a cross.

The cathedral is dedicated to Santa Maria del Fiore – Our Lady of the Flowers, as we would say in English. At the ceremonies for the dedication of the dome in 1436 (though not of its lantern, the orb and the cross, which were not completed until 1469), the leading composer of the age, Guillaume Dufay wrote a special motet for the occasion, to be performed before the Pope. It is known by its (incomplete) first line, "Nuper Rosarum Flores", which may be translated as 'When by this garland of flowers...', or perhaps, 'When by this rosary of flowers ...', since the rosary is a garland of flowers, as it is a cycle of prayer dedicated to the Virgin Mary. In part, the words of Dufay's motet read:

> Therefore, sweet parent
> Of your son, and daughter,

---

[2] Michelangelo's dome in Rome stands sixty feet higher, but in diameter and in the volume that it encloses, the dome of Sta Maria del Fiore is the larger. Hagia Sophia and the ancient dome of the Pantheon in Rome are both much lower, however impressive in their way. (Lanterns are so called because they introduce light into the dome from its very highest point.)

Virgin of virgins,

To you the Florentines

Devoted as a people,

Together in mind and body

On earth, pray to you.[3]

This dome and its lantern, its white marble buttresses and its finials, are her crown, as they are the crown of the whole city of Florence (Firenze), itself the city of the flowers.[4] There are other domes visible from a distance across Florence, most of all the dome of the Church of San Lorenzo. But this of the Cathedral is the crown.

Such a cathedral, and such a dome, could only have been built at enormous cost. I do not know if anyone has calculated its total cost. The building of it, from its foundations to its completion, took over 170 years; and during that time the construction had to be suspended, or at least slowed down, whether because of lack of money or because – after 1347 – of the terrible visitations of the plague, or because there were times when Florence itself was fighting for survival against powerful external enemies, either the threat from the Visconti of Milan or from Ladislaus, the Angevin king of Naples. And on two of the most critical of these occasions, when the fate of the city might have seemed hopeless, the Florentines were saved by what must have seemed a providential intervention: on

---

[3] At http://en.wikipedia. org/wiki/Nuper_rosarum_flores. The paradox of the Virgin Mary as both the mother and the daughter of her own son is a trope that goes back to the Middle Ages, perhaps further.

[4] Specifically, Florence is the city of the *fleur de lis*, which is its emblem, just as the *lis*, the lily, is one of the emblems of the Virgin Mary.

the first, saved from Giangaleazzo Visconti in 1402, and on the second from King Ladislaus in 1414, both of whom died suddenly in the middle of their campaign against the Florentine Republic. The construction of the Cathedral, and its funding, came to be placed in the hands of the Arte della Lana, the Wool Guild – the most important guild in the city, and the foundation of its fortunes in industry and banking. This is rightly taken to mean that its construction was closely integrated with the wealth and the well-being of the Republic. It belonged to the whole city, more than we would easily think of a large civic structure in our day – an opera house say – as *belonging* to the whole community, however proud of it we might be. This has its consequences, as we will see later in the controversies over the construction of the dome. Yet we mis-read the past if we think of it as a civic structure alone, and assume a separation between the *civis* and its sacred function and meaning. This is the cathedral of Our Lady of the Flowers, in the city of the Flowers.

But when we come down to street level, there is a difficulty with the Cathedral. Florence is apt to strike the modern visitor from the New World, or from the Antipodes, as more of a medieval city than might have been expected. Its streets are narrow, even after the Florentines themselves tried to open them up to the light and the air by at least making narrow streets out of what had been more like passage ways. There is only one view of the Cathedral at street level that I can recall. It is down the length of the Via dei Servi, from the Church of the Annunziata, looking south-eastwards. And even the Via dei Servi partially chokes off its own view. Of course, the great Dome is visible from the upper stories of the city's palazzi – as from the upper story of the Uffizi picture gallery, for example – appearing above the intervening rooves, not always quite where you expect to see it. It is only from the Piazza del Duomo itself that you suddenly come upon sufficient open space as to be able to see the Cathedral, and see it and its associated buildings all together – the Cathedral, the Baptistry of S. Giovanni (Battista) at its west end, and the free-standing bell tower (by Giotto), level with its west front.[5]

There is a still closer view of the great Dome: it is from *within* the dome itself, a way of seeing it up close, and within intimate contact with the manner of its construction. And it is of this construction that I will hereafter speak. The dome is in fact two domes, not one; and the visitor may climb, by a total of 463 steps, largely within the interior space between the two, until suddenly you emerge from its confinements out into the open air of the gallery at the base of the lantern, and the city lies out below you, visible in all directions. Seen from a distance, the dome is an elegantly pointed one (not a hemisphere); the angle of its curvature increases with its height, in what was called a *quinto acuto,* a 'pointed fifth', so called because the radius of curvature is four-fifths the width of the span to be covered. It is not until one sees the dome from close up, and from above, that you realise the increasing steepness of this curvature. From the lantern gallery, it seems to plunge down below you, so that you

---

[5] In Italy, a cathedral is often familiarly referred to as the *Duomo* (Dome) rather than as the *Cattedrale*. Note that the Florence Duomo is oriented in a west-to-east direction, as of course it should be, if it is to be 'oriented' (unlike St Peter's Basilica in Rome and many other Italian churches and cathedrals).

see, not the base of the dome on which you stand, no matter how much you lean forward, but the empty air, and the orange-red rooves far below.

At this point, some further explanation of the structure will be necessary. The ground plan of the whole cathedral is in a form of a simple Latin cross. Each of the two cross arms and the east end are built in the form of three great octagonal tribunes (as they are called), rather than ending in blank rectangular walls.[6] From the inside, they are the 'end' that does not end. From the outside, they are of the same shape, and are closed by the same terra cotta tiled semi-domes, as the great Dome itself. There is no sense of the main dome being imposed upon a building to which it does not belong. But in order to help take the great weight of the main dome, Brunelleschi – who emerged as the main architect of the construction of the dome – built four smaller structures, called exedrae, in each of the corners of the cross, in between the tribunes. From the outside, these exedrae are topped by smaller, conical rooves, rather than semi-domes; but they are all clad in the same marble, and in the same terra cotta tiles, so that the whole outward appearance is uninterrupted; and the exedrae appear to be subsidiary to the tribunes, as the tribunes are subsidiary to the great Dome itself. Together, tribunes and exedrae help take the enormous weight of the main dome, which is raised upon the four great central piers of the interior, directly over the crossing of nave and cross-arms.

It is in the exedra in the south-west corner of the angle between the southern tribune and the nave that one begins

---

6 These tribunes would form octagons were they to be completed. Three sides of the octagon are left open, so that they admit to the interior of the Cathedral as a continuous space.

the ascent, up to the Dome and the lantern. The stair case winds in a spiral up through the exedra, and then by way of the great gallery at the base of the drum up into the interior of the Dome itself. From the springing of the dome – the level from which the curvature of the dome takes off – there are three further galleries. These are interior galleries, not visible either from outside or from within the cathedral itself. They are contained entirely within the structure of the two domes, and are at successively higher levels, where one can see the great inward-curving vertical ribs, made of sandstone, that form the huge stone lattice on which the structure is built. There are twenty-four of these ribs: the eight great ribs that are visible from the outside at each of the corners of the octagon, and that pass through both domes and anchor the outer to the inner one; and two further ribs along each side, between each of them, not visible from the outside (twenty four in all). The forces exerted by such a massive structure, were they all to be downwards, might be too much for the piers beneath, even when supported by tribunes and exedrae, as they are. There was a further solution to the downward pressure, though: it lay in the shape of the dome itself. The pointed dome – rather than a hemispherical one – diverts stress *outwards*, as well as downwards. Now, the pointed dome was required by the plans, such as they were, going back to 1367, and by which all builders, or prospective builders of the cathedral, were sworn to abide. But Brunelleschi was able to turn what might have been just an irritating requirement into an advantage, structural and aesthetic. Yet even these diverted stresses need to be fixed. Brunelleschi sought to do so mainly by holding these ribs in place, external and internal ribs, by great horizontal arches, also in sandstone, that prevent them from moving laterally, or from spreading outwards. Great stone rings. In between the ribs, the structure consists of bricks, longer and harder than the house bricks we are familiar with, laid in a self-reinforcing herring bone pattern, and inclined towards the notional centre-point of the dome – the secrets of which seem not to be fully understood even to this day. Suffice it to say that they are not merely filler between the ribs, but help to carry the stresses of the dome, themselves.

As one climbs up through the inner workings of the dome, ascending by winding stone staircases from one level to the next, as the workers themselves did, the angle of the dome grows steeper, closing in towards the top; until, at the last level, you must lean forward steeply, and are definitely aware of climbing steps that rest directly upon the surface of this inner dome. In general, the dome as a structure – almost any dome – is capable of making a direct impression on you. The Pantheon in Rome, for example, in its stripped-down modern state, and with the surrounding street levels all altered, is rather a drab bulk from the outside. Once inside however, the impression is single, and awesome. But a dome also engages you intellectually. From within, the dome of the Pantheon is the like half of a great sphere, except that it is exactly as high as it is wide. There is no way that sooner or later (and probably sooner) it does not call to mind the vast curvature of the sky itself. This is just what it was intended to do since, before it was converted to a Christian church, it was a pagan temple to the planetary gods. Yet even the lay person will wonder how this or any other dome of magnitude ever stays up, because it is a structure that covers such a vast area, and without internal support. The dome is a paradoxical architecture, since it keeps itself up by itself. Or it does so, if it is built right – by stones pressing upon stones, sideways as well as downwards. Domes do fall in, sometimes soon after they are built, sometimes after a time. The dome of Hagia Sophia itself collapsed, at least in part, several times down through the centuries before Brunelleschi came to build his dome. The last major collapse had been as recently as 1346. When the Opera del Duomo (the Board of Works of the Cathedral) laid down the dimensions and regulations for the completion of the Cathedral, they could not but have known that domes, like towers, were liable to collapse. And when the visitor climbs over the highest level of Brunelleschi's structure – over the curvature of the inner dome itself – it would not be surprising if the thought were to cross your mind that Brunelleschi had better have got it right! There is only this membrane of a dome between you and the floor of the crossing, three hundred feet directly below.

He did get it right, of course. The Dome has stood for nearly seven centuries, thus far. And though there are cracks visible from the great galleries that run right round the interior of the drum (the best place from which to see the paintings in the upper dome[7]), and though some renewal of stone and wood has been necessary, the cracks that have

---

[7] These paintings are of an apocalyptic *Last Judgment,* opening through zones, ever higher to the sky. In an ascending order, they rise through the zone of Sinners, the Virtues and the Gifts of the Holy Spirit, to Mary and to Christ enthroned, ending in bands of angels and Elders. They are the work of Giorgio Vasari, Federico Zuccari and assistants, and were done in the later 16th Century. Vasari was a painter capable of covering vast areas of wall surface – as he does here. I would wish to say no more about them.

appeared are scarcely Brunelleschi's fault. Their cause seems to be a matter of on-going enquiry. They may be the result of stresses caused by the comparative weakness in the supporting drum, left by the great circular *oculi* on each of the eight sides of the octagon (the great circular 'eyes', clearly visible at a distance, from the outside of the Cathedral).[8] Or they made be the result of a slight subsidence in the south-west corner of the crossing, this subsidence itself the result of a previously undiscovered underground water-course.[9] Underground water-courses are not unknown beneath other venerable structures. And certainly, Brunelleschi did rather better than the builders of the Bell Tower of the cathedral group at Pisa, which began to tilt even while it was being built. Pisa had been one of Florence's rivals in the Tuscan region. It was then a port city, some forty miles further down the Arno, and built on the flood-plain of the river. (The coast has since extended, westwards.)

But the Opera del Duomo, the principals of the Arte della Lana, who were paying for it all, and many of the citizenry of Florence were doubtful, at every stage of the construction. By the turn of the century, the Cathedral was virtually complete, except for the southern arm, and for the vast open space where the dome should be. The Opera decided to build a drum atop the main construction (the same drum that has the oculi in it), so as to add to the amplitude and the majesty of the dome, when it should be built. Certainly it serves such a purpose.

---

[8] See e.g., Ken Maschke, "How Does it Stand? Brunelleschi's Cupola, Part 2"; at http://blogs.asce.org/bridgingthegap/2012/01/03

[9] See Eugenio Battisti, *Brunelleschi: The Complete Work*. Thames & Hudson, London, 1981, Ch. 8, pp.156-7 and n.

There is a well known fresco in the Spanish Chapel of the nearby Church of Sta Maria Novella, by one Andrea di Bonaiuoto, and painted sometime in the 1390s. The painting itself is not particularly distinguished; its interest lies in its representation of the great Cathedral as it was envisaged when it should be complete. What is significant for present purposes is that it represents the Cathedral with its planned dome, but without the intervening drum, and one can immediately see the difference. The dome of Bonaiuoto's picture sits more squat, more insignificant, than the dome as it came to be built. When Michelangelo came to design the dome of St Peter's, good Florentine as he was, he had the Dome of Florence continually in mind: *he* included a drum – and so did all the builders of great domes thereafter. Sir Christopher Wren's St Paul's has one, plus a smaller, higher one resting on top of it, as if the smaller drum might be telescoped within the larger one – as a famous, and influential, small circular church built by Bramante on the supposed site of St Peter's crucifixion (known as the Tempietto) does. The Capitol building in Washington also has two – though note in passing that the Capitol's is not a masonry dome, but a cast iron one. All such domes conduct a kind of conversation with one another, across time and distance.

The trouble is that though the drum of Sta Maria del Fiore looks 'right', it not only postponed for them the problem of how to actually build the dome, it increased the difficulty of doing so. And of this, the Opera and the citizens of Florence were well aware. The eyes of the world were on them – or at least, the eyes of the world as they thought of it. As Antonio Manetti, the probable author of the earliest of the biographies of Brunelleschi, wrote:

> ... If that which was meant to create honor did not come out well at the fourteen *braccia* level [of the drum], it would be shameful, and the *operai* and consuls of the Wool Guild and all the members would be disgraced throughout the world and the rest of the city even more.[10]

There was the example of Pisa, to the west, with the same kind of grouping of Cathedral, Baptistry, and Campanile as Florence – quite beautiful in its old fashioned, 'gothic' way. But not only did the Campanile (the Bell Tower) still lean, its angle of inclination was actually getting worse. And there was the further example of Siena, Florence's bitter enemy to the south. The Sienese had started to build a cathedral on such a scale as they would never complete. The Black Death devastated Siena even more than it did Florence; and Siena never recovered from the disaster, either in population or in wealth. Large as it is, the present Cathedral of Siena was to have been but one of the cross-arms of the Cathedral as they intended it.

Domes, as they were built in the West, required wooden centring. This centring would both support the structure as it was being built – since domes only support

---

[10] Antonio Manetti, *Life of Brunelleschi*, ed. Howard Saalman, & transl. Catherine Enggass; Pennsylvania State University Press, 1970, p.78. Manetti's biography is thought to have been written in the 1480s – Brunelleschi himself died in 1446. The *braccia* was a measurement of about two feet length. The word actually means the measurement of an *arm's* length, roughly from the elbow to the tip of the hand. (Dressmakers will be familiar with such a rough calculation.)

themselves once they are completed – and serve to guide the builders as to the angle of curvature. But the dome of Santa Maria del Fiore would have to begin at a height somewhere about 180 feet above the floor of the Cathedral, and cover a span of about 140 feet in diameter. No such trees existed as could provide the timbering for such a centring. As Manetti tells it, the *operai* must have been desperate; their ancestors had left them with a seemingly insoluble problem:

> From Filippo's words [Brunelleschi's] the *operai* unanimously drew the conclusion that a large building of such a character could not be completed and that it had been naïve of earlier masters and those who relied on them to believe [it].[11]

When they could delay no longer, the *operai* took Brunelleschi's advice and, in 1418, called a great conference of architects, engineers, stonemasons, and carpenters, and anyone else who might have a theory about how to build it. There is a story as told by Manetti – and re-told by Giorgio Vasari, in his *Lives of the Artists* – of one such theorist who actually proposed raising an artificial hill on the floor of the Cathedral crossing, and erecting the centring on top of it. And like the Irish farmer who proposed ploughing his field by burying turnips and turning his pigs loose on it, this anonymous theorist proposed burying money in his hill and turning the children of Florence onto it, once the dome had been completed. Stories like this must have been told on the streets of Florence for generations – talked about, and guffawed over.

---

[11] Saalman, *op.cit.*, p.66.

Only Brunelleschi himself seemed to be confident in his solution. And yet his solution seemed only a measure less absurd. He would build the dome, first by building not one dome, but two – one inside the other. It would baffle sheer common sense. His theory was that by doing so, the total weight of both together would be reduced. The outer dome would act as an outer membrane so as to take the weather and protect the inner structure from storm and lightning (and impart to the dome a more 'magnificent' profile). Secondly, he proposed to build the dome with no centring at all, but rather by means of scaffolding anchored into the rising structure, and building it in ascending rings of masonry, rather than by curving surfaces hanging out into empty space. It must have seemed like pulling yourself up by your own bootstraps. Each ring would be firmly set in place before the next one would be built on top of it, the rings slowly drawn in to the top – though the notion is easier to conceive of than actually to do.

Though neither of his biographers, neither Manetti nor Vasari, liked to speak ill of their subjects, Brunelleschi must have been a difficult man. He was in person, small and insignificant. And he kept his cards close to his chest, so to speak, both because he was by temperament a natural born isolate, who thought long and hard, and did not like to talk about it, and because he lived in a time and a place where, as he well knew, others would steal his ideas. Here he was, faced by the necessity of explaining to the Opera how he might do what others could not conceive of, yet at the same time protect himself from those others who would say that they had thought of *that* too, once he had explained it.

A young Sienese engineer named Mariano Taccola once recorded a conversation with Brunelleschi that Giovanni Battisti, who prints it in his book on Brunelleschi, thinks could not have taken place earlier than 1433, and perhaps in 1436 or 1440, and perhaps as late as 1446, when Brunelleschi might have passed through Siena – in other words, when Brunelleschi was already famous as the builder of the dome:

> Do not tell everybody about your ideas [Brunelleschi tells him] but speak only to the few who understand and appreciate science, because putting yourself about too much and explaining your own inventions and actions is just squandering your own talent. There are many who love to listen only in order to criticize those who do new things, and to contradict what they make and say, so as to prevent them from being heard in high places and by the right authority. And after a few months they will go about saying the same things or writing them down or putting them into their own drawings, and they will boast with utter presumption of being themselves the inventors of the very things they had first scoffed at, and will not hesitate to appropriate the glory belonging to others. And there are thickheaded and ignorant types who, whenever they hear some new idea or invention that they never thought of before, will at once call the inventor crazy and his theories ridiculous. 'For God's sake, shut up,' they say, 'or everyone will think you're a fool.' But don't be browbeaten by those who speak ill of you out of envy and ignorance to waste the talents that God has given you. Pursue them, exercise them in

such a way that you will be held wise by the wise,
through your virtue and your mind."[12]

There may be some re-creation of a remembered
conversation involved here; and yet a young man such as
Taccola was, given advice by one of the most famous men
of his country and his age, is likely to have noted it down,
especially when the advice seemed to bear the fruits
of long, and perhaps bitter, experience. The historical
record does not otherwise provide us with what sounds
so much like the authentic voice of Brunelleschi the man
as this does. And his candour as well as his pungency of
expression is notable. Manetti, who would also have been
a young man when he knew Brunelleschi, as Taccola was,
remembers Brunelleschi telling him that at the height of
the controversy he was reluctant even to walk the streets
of Florence for fear that people were talking about him
behind his back. He was twice even physically carried
out of the council room where the *operai* and the consuls
of the Wool Guild were conferring on the problem for
talking nonsense.

And it was long before the Opera would completely
trust him. At first, they gave the task jointly to two others,
as well as to him. All three jointly were to be *capomaestri*
(literally, headmasters). One of these, Battista D'Antonio,
does not concern us further. He seems to have been more
of a construction overseer than what we would think of
as an architect. But the other one, Lorenzo Ghiberti, was
another matter. Ghiberti and Brunelleschi had a history.
Ghiberti was the sculptor of the much admired great

---

[12] The conversation exists only in a single manuscript, in the Bayerische
Staatsbibliothek in Munich. This translation is given in Eugenio
Battisti, *op. cit.*, pp. 20-21.

bronze doors of the Church of San Giovanni, the ancient and venerable Baptistry church[13] that stands before the main entrance of the Cathedral, and is dedicated to one of the other patron saints of the City. It is no accident that the Cathedral itself echoes San Giovanni in its repeated octagonal shapes (San Giovanni is hexagonal), in its dome within a dome (San Giovanni has a hexagonal dome beneath its outer, conical roof), in its roof tiling, and in the lantern that sits atop of it.

In 1401 – some twenty years earlier – Brunelleschi and Ghiberti had been in effect the finalists in a competition for the design of a new set of doors for San Giovanni in the same manner as the first set, by Andrea Pisano, from some seventy years earlier. Each door was to be divided into small panels, about 20 inches by 18. Andrea's doors told the story of John the Baptist (appropriately enough) in high relief sculpture. For the competition, seven sculptors from Florence and from Tuscany were chosen by their general repute. They were given a stipend, and sufficient metal to make a single panel, all of them on the same subject – the Sacrifice of Isaac – and twelve months in which to complete it. I presume the subject was chosen because it was considered a type from the Old Testament of Christ's own sacrifice in the New, and because the overall narrative subject of the new doors was to be the Life of Christ. Christ by his death completed Abraham's (averted) sacrifice of his own son, Isaac. But all this was in the year 1401; and within months, the subject took on a startling new relevance for the Florentines, who were at war with Milan: Giangaleazzo Visconti himself was to die

---

[13] They thought at the time that it might even date back to the Romans.

within the year – and to the Florentines, this was another story of miraculous intervention from above such as the story of Abraham and Isaac was.

By common consent, the panels of two of the contestants, Brunelleschi and Ghiberti, were clearly superior to the others. But the judges were unable to decide between them, and awarded the commission for the new doors to both of them, jointly; and Brunelleschi would have none of working on a project with someone else – and perhaps, not Ghiberti especially. As Manetti tells it, Brunelleschi finished his panel promptly, and then put it away till the judging should call for it. Ghiberti on the other hand, and perhaps by deliberate strategy, unable to get a sight of Brunelleschi's panel, deliberately consulted widely while he was working on his own panel, including with those who were to be the judges. They already well knew his panel when they came to judge it, and could scarcely retract their lavish praise of it when the time came to see Brunelleschi's panel, which took them by surprise, presumably with its superior sense of drama as well as its general craftsmanship in managing metal.[14] Hence their decision to award the commission jointly to both of them. But if Brunelleschi were not to be the outright winner of it, then he made it clear that he would rather it be awarded to his rival. Vasari, who also tells the story, makes of it a gesture of magnanimity towards a rival whose merits he freely recognized. But

---

[14] Both panels survive, and are now held in the Bargello museum in Florence. When I would show students reproductions of them, they too were divided as to which was best. (By a small margin, they preferred Ghiberti's as being more graceful, more beautiful.)

it is possible to see how his motives are capable of quite other interpretation.

Afterwards, Brunelleschi disappeared from Florence altogether, as he seems to have been wont to do from time to time. In fact, he sold a small family farm and took himself off to Rome, where his interests and his solitary researches gradually shifted from sculpture to the close study of Roman architecture, or to what remained of it. There in Rome, digging among the ruins, closely studying the Pantheon and such standing monuments, he began to recognize, anew, the Orders of ancient architecture as no-one else had yet done. And he taught himself, by piecemeal and by patience, the Roman methods of joining stone to stone, and brick to brick; and by detective work, how such stones could have been lifted into place, and the tackle that would have been required to do it – a work as remarkable for its imagination as for its close observation, and for its physical/mechanical understanding. As Manetti and Vasari well understood, it was all of it a preparation for a task not yet conceived of, except by God.

But all of this was twenty years previous. And now, when it came to the construction of the Dome, the whole situation seemed to be repeating itself. Here he was, shackled with the same Lorenzo Ghiberti, who may have been his superior as a sculptor, but who did not even know what he was ignorant of, as an architect and engineer.

The two fought a kind of duel of wits on the construction site, now on the ground (where Brunelleschi himself lived), now high in the air, hundreds of feet above. At a critical stage in the construction, where the dome was required to begin to draw inwards, Brunelleschi complained of being

Brunelleschi's Dome

ill, and took to his bed so that Ghiberti should be forced, if
not to admit, then to *show* that he did not really know how
to go on. Work ceased while the masons and bricklayers
waited for instructions. They turned to Ghiberti, who told
them, or intimated to them, that though he knew what to
do, he would do nothing without his *co-capomaestro*, and
sent them off to Brunelleschi. For his part, Brunelleschi
either was, or claimed to be, too ill to attend to such
matters, and referred them back to Ghiberti, who after all
was drawing the same salary as he was. The result was
that Ghiberti was manoeuvred into doing some of the
immediately needful work on his own, and at last revealed
his limitations – undeniably, since some of his work had
to be undone at great expense.

Thereafter, Brunelleschi became in effect the chief
architect and engineer of the project. Henry Saalman
doubts the story because he can find nothing in the record
of such an interruption to the work. But I find too much of
the nature and the character of the man, Brunelleschi, in
it; and the roots of the story reach too far back into their
past to be doubted. Ghiberti's supporters spread the word
that Brunelleschi shammed illness because he himself
did not know how to go on with the work, or was afraid
to do so. Well yes, that is exactly what they would say,
when you stop to think about it, were it actually to have
happened. Though Ghiberti was retained thereafter (and
not dismissed, as some accounts say), Brunelleschi's salary
was much increased for the remainder of the project; and
in the popular mind, the Dome became *his* Dome.

One hundred years later, in Vasari's *Lives*[15],

[15] A two-volume selection of Giorgio Vasari's *Lives of the Artists* is
available in Penguin. The Life of Brunelleschi is in Vol. 1.

Brunelleschi became the very type of the new Artist As Genius, who by virtue of his distinct difference from other people and from received ways of thinking, working alone in mind and soul, answerable if not solely to himself then to God, was to perform wonders. Vasari was something of a proponent of and a publicist for the New Age of wonders that we know as the Renaissance. He was concerned that the artist should be accepted as a thinker, and not as a mere craftsman. And here, in Brunelleschi, was a man who thought long and hard, and often about things that others had not yet begun to think about – had not even begun to conceive of as a subject for thought. Vasari himself was so completely of the New Age that he and his book did so much to establish that he was blind or indifferent to the causes, artistic and social, of the contention that Brunelleschi so often found himself in. The community was paying for this project (as they paid for the great bronze doors of San Giovanni); and they went on doing so, through plague, through economic recession, and through war, even when the Republic itself was in peril. Little wonder that their interest in it was acute, excited, and continuous. Medieval cathedrals are not known by the name of their builders. That is because their construction was a sacred and a communal achievement. But this Dome – if not the whole Cathedral of Santa Maria del Fiore – was now Brunelleschi's Dome. For better and worse, the new type of the Artist had well and truly arrived. Not that Brunelleschi himself had any such intentions. He had always gone his own way.

BRIGHT SHOOTS OF EVERLASTINGNESS
Henry Vaughan and His Poetry

Brian Coman

Incised in stone above the west door of the little Gothic church at Staunton Harold, Leicestershire, is the following inscription:

In the yeare 1653

When all things Sacred were throughout ye nation

Either demolisht or profaned

Sir Robert Shirley, Barronet,

Founded this church;

Whose singular praise it is,

To have done the best things in ye worst times,

and

Hoped them in the most callamitous

The righteous shall be had in everlasting remembrance.

We are told that Sir Robert Shirley, a Royalist, had refused to assist Cromwell. He was sent to the Tower and died there, aged twenty-seven. These were strife-torn times. The Civil War had ended in victory for the Parliamentarian cause in 1646 and the Monarchy did not return until 1660. It was during those same strife-torn times that Henry Vaughan 'The Silurist' wrote his most memorable poetry and it might be said of him, also, that he 'done the best things in the worst times'. Vaughan, a Welshman, was born in Breconshire at Newton-upon-Usk in 1621 and died in 1695, not far from his birthplace. The Civil War was to have a very important influence on both the man and his poetry.

Today, Vaughan is chiefly remembered as one of the so-called 'metaphysical poets' of the 17th C. The other important members of the group are Donne, Crashaw, Cowley, Herbert, Marvell, and Traherne. The term 'metaphysical' seems to have been invented by John Dryden but was made famous by Dr Johnson who first used it to describe a type of poetry employing unusual and paradoxical images, relying on intellectual wit and upon learned imagery and subtle argument. For Johnson, it was meant as a pejorative term:

> Their thoughts are often new, but seldom natural; they are not obvious, but neither are they just; and the reader, far from wondering that he missed them, wonders more frequently by what perverseness of industry they were ever found. [*Lives of the Poets*: Cowley]

Such a judgement from an 18th century critic is hardly surprising. In an age that placed all of its hope on human reason and Baconian science, the highly imaginative poetry of the preceding century was largely dismissed as a 'conceit'[1]. Indeed, even in Henry Vaughan's own times, allegorical habits of mind were being replaced by more realistic ones (Bacon published his *Novum Organum* the year before Henry Vaughan was born) and, in this sense, Vaughan's poetry looks back towards the Middle

---

[1] The word did not yet bear its current meaning (though it was on its way to doing so). It still bore its older meaning of 'concept'. Used pejoratively, it meant a poetry of clever ideas.

Ages rather than to his own times. Fortunately both literary tastes and philosophical opinions were to change again in later times. In the early 20th C, both Ezra Pound and T.S. Eliot were to discover deep affinities with the 'metaphysicals' and today, their poetry is well represented in most anthologies of English verse. It was in his essay on the metaphysical poets [1921] that Eliot made his now famous suggestion of a 'dissociation of sensibility' that marked the end of what we might call the metaphysical style. The basis of this style, Eliot thought, was the poet's ability to constantly amalgamate disparate experiences to form new wholes. The metaphysical poet 'possessed a mechanism of sensibility which could devour any kind of experience'. It is with Milton and Dryden – those giants of the 17th Century – Eliot suggests, that we see this 'dissociation of sensibility' come to the fore and to manifest itself in the work of later poets such as Collins, Gray, Goldsmith and the great Dr Johnson himself. The language of these poets may have become more refined, but (so Eliot thought) the feeling had become more crude.

As so it was that, after more than two centuries of virtual obscurity, the poetry of Henry Vaughan came to be valued again. Between 1679 and 1847, there was no new edition of Vaughan although one of his poems had been anthologized as early as 1803. But, if influential modern critics like Eliot and Pound had some hand in restoring the fortunes of the 'metaphysicals', so much more so did the *Zeitgeist* – by the time Eliot died (1965) the bankruptcy of positivism was clearly in evidence. Given that Edmund Blunden had written on Vaughan in 1927 and Siegfried Sassoon had visited Vaughan's grave and penned a sonnet on that visit in 1928, we might regard these poets as early prophets who, in the wake of the Great War, perhaps foresaw a re-emergence of interest in the imaginative and allegorical as a sort of counter reaction to the Slough of Despond which had developed out of the hell of Flanders. One might see the emergence of a wider and more general interest in Blake's poetry in the same light, although W.B.Yeats and Edwin Ellis first edited Blake's work in 1891-3.

Insofar as the poet himself is concerned, as distinct from the poetry, we owe the resurrection of Henry Vaughan in large part to two grand ladies of literary leanings, the Misses Louise Guiney and Gwenllian Morgan. Miss Morgan was a 'local', so to speak, and lived most of her long life in Breconshire, dying there in 1939 in her 88th year. The daughter of a local pastor, she was a keen historian, and intensely interested in Vaughan. She was also the first woman in Wales to serve the office of mayor. Miss Guiney, by contrast, was an American Catholic, with no close connection to Wales. She was, nonetheless, an ardent Anglophile, with a particular love for the Royalist poets and a sympathy for the Royalist cause.[2] Morgan and Guiney gathered together what

---

[2] Such intensity of feeling some 250 years later may seem a little odd, but is by no means unique. I am indebted to John Julius Norwich for the following pieces which appeared consecutively in the *In Memoriam* column of *The Times* in London on 3rd Sept., 1969:

> OLIVER CROMWELL, 25th April, 1599 – 3rd September 1658. Lord Protector, 1653-1658. Statesman, General and Ruler.
> 'Let God arise, let His enemies be scattered'. Psalm 68, verse i.
> In honoured remembrance.
> CROMWELL. – To the eternal condemnation of Oliver, Seditionist, Traitor, Regicide, Racialist, proto-Fascist and blasphemous Bigot. God save England from his like. – Hugo Ball.

scant information we have today concerning the life of Henry Vaughan. Unfortunately, both these ladies died before they were able to publish their biography of Vaughan. That task was taken up by F.E. Hutchinson, an Anglican Divine and onetime chaplain of Kings College, who published his account (heavily reliant on Morgan & Guiney's researches) in 1947.[3] One other biography has appeared since then, that of Stevie Davies in 1995.[4] Her account, though, introduces no new material and is largely concerned with a personal appreciation of the poet.

It is perhaps something of a blessing that we know relatively little about Vaughan the man for this has largely spared us those usual, weighty volumes where the minutiae of daily life are drawn into interminable discussion regarding 'influences' on poetic production. We have no images of him, no descriptions of his personality, and only a fairly sketchy record of his time on this earth. Even so, I note that Stevie Davies has a whole chapter ('The Crucible of Twinship') where an elaborate superstructure of critical analysis and comment rests on the scant knowledge we have of the relationship between Henry Vaughan and his twin brother, Thomas.

Of Vaughan's early life we know virtually nothing save that he and his twin brother were taught at a nearby school by one Matthew Herbert, an Anglican clergyman. Later, Henry Vaughan may have attended Oxford University although the records establish only that his twin brother did. Whatever the case, he certainly went to London and

---

[3] *Henry Vaughan: A Life and Interpretation.* Oxford Univ. Press. London. 1947. 260pp.

[4] *Henry Vaughan.* Seren (Poetry Wales Press), Border Lines Series. Bridgend, Wales, 1995. 213pp.

seems to have studied law for a period. With the outbreak of the Civil War, he returned home and there, for a short time, was secretary to Sir Marmaduke Lloyd, chief justice of the sessions. We know that Vaughan was married to Catherine Wise by 1646 and that the couple had four children. Catherine appears to have died very young, almost certainly within a decade of the marriage. Vaughan married again, probably around 1655. His second wife, Elizabeth, was his former wife's sister and she too, bore him four children.

The question whether Henry Vaughan bore arms in the Civil War has been much discussed. Hutchinson is of the view that Henry did take up arms for the Royalists, but Vaughan's first modern editor, H.F. Lyte (1847) took an opposite view. Whatever the truth of the matter, there can be no doubt that the defeat of the Royalists, together with the death of his younger brother, William (in 1648), had a profound effect on him. This is evidenced by the sudden change in both the nature and the quality of the poetry he wrote.

As to his profession in later adult life, there are indications that he may have been a doctor but little evidence of any training in this field. In a letter to John Aubrey in 1673, Vaughan talks about his brother, Thomas, and then says: 'My profession also is physic which I have practised now for many years with good success ...'. Earlier (1640s), Vaughan was probably employed as a secretary to Judge Lloyd (and soon after, Hutchinson surmises, as a soldier).

With this brief biography serving as a sort of introduction, we turn now to the poetry. His first volume of poetry, *Poems with the Tenth Satire of Juvenal Englished*, was published in 1646. A second volume, entitled *Olor Iscanus* (Swan of the Usk) appears to have been completed by 1647, but was not published until 1651. It is in this second volume that Vaughan gives himself the title of 'Silurist' – a reference to the ancient tribe, the Silures, which inhabited the south-east of Wales and which was mentioned by Tacitus as having caused the invading Romans a good deal of trouble. I assume that the Silures also gave us the geological term 'Silurian'.

Of the bulk of these early poems, perhaps the less said the better. They are largely very conventional, secular poems, often imitating earlier poets such as Habington or Randolph. I think it fair to say that if Vaughan's reputation rested on these alone, he would be largely forgotten today. The first volume includes a number of love poems, almost all of which are addressed to *Amoret*, a sort of generic title for the female subject. Here, Vaughan follows earlier poets such as Lovelace, Browne, Lodge and Waller. Nonetheless, some of the poetry is memorable. Here, for instance, is a little vignette of the London of Vaughan's student days:

> Should we go now a wandering, we should meet
> With catchpoles, whores, & carts in every street:
> Now when each narrow lane, each nook & cave,
> Sign-posts, & shop-doors, pimp for every knave,
> When riotous sinful plush, and tell-tale spurs
> Walk Fleet street, & the Strand, when the soft stirs
> Of bawdy, ruffled silks, turn night to day;
> And the loud whip, and coach scolds all the way;

> When lusts of all sorts, and each itchy blood
>
> From the Tower-wharf to Cymbeline, and Lud,
>
> Hunts for a mate, and the tired footman reels
>
> 'Twixt chair-men, torches, & the hackney wheels...
>
> *A Rhapsody (lines 35-46)*

Here is a picture of the seamier side of London, with that sort of eye for all the sordid detail which we might expect of Hogarth or Dickens. The phrases 'riotous sinful plush' and bawdy, ruffled silks' are particularly well contrived.

The second volume of Vaughan's poetry is somewhat more adventuresome and treats a wide range of themes. It includes translations of Ovid, Ausonius, Boethius and Casimir. Looking at the index in Alan Rudrum's splendidly annotated edition of Vaughan's poems[5], one cannot help but notice how the lengthy titles, often overweighed with effusive praise of their respective human subjects, contrast with the short, pithy titles of the later religious poetry (and, indeed, many of the religious poems are untitled). Thus we find, for instance:

> *To the Truly Noble, and Most Excellently Accomplished,*
> *the Lord Kildare Digby*

and

> *An Elegy on the Death of Mr R.W. Slain in the Late*
> *Unfortunate Differences at Rowton Heath, near Chester, 1645*

One has the impression that the poem has, in each case,

---

[5] *Henry Vaughan. The Complete Poems.* Penguin Books, London. 1983 Revised Edition. 718pp. All extracts of poems quoted in this essay come from Rudrum's Edition.

occasioned less literary effort than the title! For my own part, when I read these titles I cannot help but compare them to the equally ponderous titles so beloved of the Pre-Raphaelite Brotherhood for their paintings. My second example from Vaughan, for instance, bears comparison with Holman Hunt:

> *Rienzi Vowing to Obtain Justice for the Death of his Young Brother, Slain in a Skirmish between the Colonna and Orsini Factions.*

But perhaps in *Olor Iscanus*, we should particularly note Vaughan's choice in translating Ovid, Ausonius, Boethius and Casimir. If, as some commentators suspect, Vaughan translated his selections in the order given here, then we see a gradual progression towards more serious philosophical and religious themes. Casimir (Mathias Casimir Sarbiewski) was a Polish Jesuit whose poetry often addressed religious themes. We might also expect that, in his reading of Ausonius, Vaughan would have learned of Paulinus of Nola at this time. Later (1654), Vaughan was to publish a rather free translation of the *Life of Paulinus* by Rosweyde.

As I foreshadowed earlier in this essay, the events associated with the Civil War, combined with the death of his younger brother were to have a profound effect on Vaughan and his poetry. Other commentators have also suggested that Vaughan himself may have endured some serious illness at about this time and that such illness brought the fact of human mortality sharply into focus. As Dr. Johnson once said, 'when a man knows he is to be hanged in a fortnight, it concentrates his mind wonderfully'! Irrespective of which of these influences assumed the most importance in the mind of the poet, what we see in the poems of his 1650 edition, titled *Silex Scintillans*, is a virtual transformation. Even if Vaughan's earlier acquaintance with the work of Casimir (and, perhaps, other and earlier Christian writers) is taken into account, there is nothing to prepare the reader for what F.E. Hutchinson calls the 'heightened feeling and majestic utterance' that we get in so many of the poems of *Silex Scintillans*.

From the lovesick, young gallant who pens his rather conventional, foppish, and formulaic verses to Amoret, we come to this:

> I saw Eternity the other night
>
> Like a great Ring of pure and endless light,
>
> All calm, as it was bright,
>
> And round beneath it, Time in hours, days, years
>
> Driven by the spheres
>
> Like a vast shadow mov'd, In which the world
>
> And all her train were hurl'd.
>
> *(The World)*

Hutchinson is in no two minds about what has happened to the poet. He refers to it as a conversion. This, I think, is a little too dramatic. There can be no question regarding the sudden new direction in Vaughan's poetry, but he was always a believing Christian. He was not converted to Christianity, but simply lifted to a higher plane of spiritual understanding. This is very obvious when one considers the subject matter of his religious poetry. Alan Rudrum's notes to the *Silex Scintillans* poems run to well over 100 pages of tight text. The vast majority of the references are biblical ones, some quite obscure, and we can only conclude that Vaughan had a prodigious knowledge of the Bible. Such knowledge does not come abruptly with conversion but is the fruit of years and years of reading. The raw materials were surely latent in Vaughan and, as he himself says in his introduction to the first *Silex Scintillans* volume, what ignited his poetic imagination was the divine flash of the Spirit on a reluctant and hardened heart:

> You have attempted many times, I admit, to capture me without injury, and your voice, haunting me, has endeavored without words to make me heedful. A more divine breath has entreated me with its gentle action and admonished me in vain with its holy murmur. I was flint – deaf and silent ... You draw nearer and break that mass which is my rocky heart, and that which was formerly stone is now made flesh. See how it is torn, its fragments at last setting your heavens alight ... [6]

These fiery sparks from the heart constitute the best of Vaughan's poetry. In poem after poem of the *Silex Scintillans* collections (1650 and 1655), we have that direct evidence of a man who

> ... felt through all this fleshly dress
>
> Bright shoots of everlastingness.
>
> *(The Retreat)*

A few short extracts may serve to give something of

[6] Here I use part of the translation by Alan Rudrum of Vaughan's Latin original.

the flavour for those who are not familiar with Vaughan's poetry:

> When first I saw true beauty, and thy joys
> Active as light, and calm without all noise
> Shined on my soul, I felt through all my powers
> Such a rich air of sweets, as evening showers
> Fanned by a gentle gale convey and breathe
> On some parched bank, crowned with a flowery wreath;
> Odours, and myrrh, and balm in one rich flood …
> *(Mount of Olives, II)*

> They are all gone into the world of light!
> And I alone sit ling'ring here;
> Their very memory is fair and bright,
> And my sad thoughts doth clear.

> It glows and glitters in my cloudy breast
> Like stars upon some gloomy grove,
> Or those faint beams in which this hill is dressed,
> After the sun's remove.
> *('They are all gone into the world of light!')*

> My soul, there is a country
> Far beyond the stars,
> Where stands a winged sentry
> All skillful in the wars,
> There, above noise, and danger
> Sweet peace sits crowned with smiles,

And one born in a manger

Commands the beauteous files ...

(Peace)

The themes treated by Vaughan in these poems have been the subject of much scholarly questioning over the last eighty years or so. To what extent was Vaughan influenced by the Hermetic Philosophy? To what extent was he influenced by Platonism? Was Vaughan a true mystic and, if so, did he follow the *via negativa* or the *via positiva*? Was Vaughan a true 'nature poet' in the sense of being a precursor to the English Romantic poets? Here, I cannot attempt to deal in any detail with all of these 'problems' which the critics see in Vaughan's religious poetry. However, a few general comments might help to resolve some of these supposed difficulties or, at least, put them into some sort of perspective.

In the first place, it is absolutely clear that Henry Vaughan is a Christian traditionalist in his religious outlook. This is not to suppose that he does not bring in ideas from the Platonists and Neoplatonists, or from Hermeticism, but rather, that he assimilates such ideas within a thoroughly traditional, Christian framework. If Vaughan's Christianity appears a little 'unorthodox', it is perhaps because he is a man out of his time – his religion often tends to look back toward what he saw as more primitive but purer expressions of Christianity. We need to remember that the Civil War cast Vaughan adrift from his traditional church environment and he was forced to find his own expression of Christianity. In so doing, he borrowed freely from many traditions, both within pre-Civil War Anglicanism and further afield. The religious poetry of George Herbert, for instance, was to exert an enormous influence upon him, and he freely acknowledges his debt to Herbert in some of his poems.

With regard to Platonic influences, many possible correlates present themselves in the poetry. The first is the theme of childhood. In what is probably Vaughan's most famous poem, *The Retreat,* he begins:

> Happy those early days! when I
> Shined in my Angel-infancy.

Here is the clear notion, not only of childhood innocence, but also of childhood understanding and acceptance of the spiritual realm. This theme appears in many of Vaughan's poems. It is tempting to suppose that Vaughan alludes to the Platonic notion of anamnesis and pre-existence and, indeed, that may have been an influence upon him. We ought to remember, though, that Vaughan was a man who knew his Bible backwards and it is more likely that he had in mind that injunction in Matthew 18.3: 'Verily I say unto you, Except ye be converted, and become as little children, ye shall not enter into the kingdom of heaven' (KJV).

Another clear debt to Platonism comes from Vaughan's notion of a cosmos of spheres or rings with ordered motion, and we tend to immediately associate this with Plato. One peculiarity of Vaughan in this respect is his association of ordered motion with silence. Time after time we get that notion of the profound beauty of silence. When he saw eternity (*The World, I*) it was:

> All calm, as it was bright

Of the stars (*The Constellation*), he says:

Fair, ordered lights (whose motion without noise
Resembles those true joys …)

And, perhaps his most beautiful depiction of the Platonic Beauty (*Mount of Olives II*):

When first I saw true beauty, and thy joys
Active as light, and calm without all noise

There are, of course, other echoes of Platonism or Neo-Platonism in Vaughan's poetry but, very often, they have come down to him from that earlier Christian tradition drawing upon the Augustinian world-picture. The idea of this world as an imperfect image of the real world leads naturally to the concept of *contemptus mundi*, implicit in Augustine and so evident in much of Vaughan's work. Indeed, Vaughan's translation of the *De Contemptu Mundi* of St. Eucherius of Lyon (5th C) is, as far as this writer is aware, the only English translation of the work. But it would be wrong to suppose that Vaughan or, for that matter, Augustine, regarded matter as evil, or deprecated the created order. Quite the reverse in Vaughan's case. He saw all plants and animals as responding to the Divine, and even lifeless stones paid a sort of tribute to their Maker ('By some hid sense their Maker gave').

Vaughan's association with the Hermetic philosophy is based upon certain direct evidence in the poems themselves as well as the fact that his twin brother, Thomas, delved into alchemy and was well acquainted with the writings attributed to 'Thrice-Great Hermes'. In his published work, Thomas also quotes from Paracelsus, Robert Fludd and Cornelius Agrippa. Nonetheless, Thomas saw himself as 'neither Papist nor Sectary but a true, resolute Protestant in the best sense of the Church of England'. Despite these assertions by Thomas, his writings on alchemy do suggest a more erratic and headstrong approach to the subject matter than his brother, Henry who, as Hutchinson says,

> passed the Hermetic ideas and terms so integrally into the common language of Christian tradition that they do not disconcert the reader; they are not resented as the technical terms of an unfamiliar way of expressing his conviction of the 'commerce' between heaven and earth.

Other authors, though, believe that Hermetic influences are much more important in Henry Vaughan's work than that assumed by a simple borrowing of Hermetic terms to illustrate or 'flesh out' an otherwise conventional, Christian understanding. Miss Elizabeth Holmes devoted a whole book to the subject, and it has been discussed by many other commentators.[7] And yet, Vaughan's supposed Hermeticism is very difficult to pin down. It appears as only scattered references throughout the corpus of his work and, in the end, one tends to agree with Ross Garner who says (of Vaughan's supposed Hermeticism):

> Vaughan does not make out of God a scientific principle, an adjunct of matter by which it may be governed. He takes explanations of the physical universe of which he is aware and uses them parabolically to adumbrate Christian doctrine.[8]

And so, while we may come across references to Hermetic terms such as *signatures, rays, beams,*

---

[7] *Henry Vaughan and the Hermetic Philosophy.* Oxford, 1932.

[8] *Henry Vaughan: Experience and the Tradition.* Univ. Chicago Press, 1959.

sympathies, magnets, and so on, these are terms which Vaughan assimilates effortlessly into his Christianity..

For all that, the words that crop up most frequently in Vaughan's *Silex Scintillans* poems are biblical words – shoots, buds, dew, doves, stones, roses, light, to mention but a few of his favourite themes. There can be little doubt that Vaughan's main source is the Bible and that other influences are secondary by comparison. But the word *white*, so often used by Vaughan as an epithet for what he holds in high regard (e.g., 'white, celestial thought' in *The Retreat*)), is probably not of biblical origin and deserves special mention. Hutchinson points out that the Welsh counterpart, *gwyn,* signifies not only white but fair, happy, holy, blessed. 'There is', he says 'no more frequent epithet in Welsh poetry'. As an example, he goes on to point out that the Welsh word for Paradise is *gwynfyd* – literally 'white world'.

The question of Vaughan's mysticism is also problematical. Very often, you will see Vaughan (and Traherne for that matter) described in anthologies of English poetry as 'a Seventeenth century mystic' It's not that easy, for there are mystics and mystics. If we are talking of a person who has achieved a full unity with the Divine – a man, as it were, living wholly in another world – then Vaughan was not a mystic. For one thing, there are practical considerations which are not lost on Stevie Davies in her account of Vaughan's life. She wonders (and so do I) how someone with eight children by two marriages manages to get enough 'quiet time' to meditate at all! Most of Vaughan's important religious poetry was written before he was thirty-five years old, and between

77

his twenty-fifth and thirty-fifth year, four children were born into the Vaughan household. The house would have been a fairly lively place, certainly no eremite's cell. Moreover, either as a secretary or a doctor, we assume that Vaughan had to earn a crust. Mind you, J.S. Bach was in the same boat, but I note that no less a critic than H.C. Robbins-Landon has described him as being 'in many respects a genuine mystic'.[9]

More likely, I think, is Ross Garner's appraisal. In discussing one of Vaughan's better known 'mystical' poems, *The Night*, he supposes that what characterises Vaughan's religious experience is that of a *longing* for mystical union, not its achievement. And yet, when we read his great religious poems, is it not the case that we, ourselves, *feel* as if Vaughan has achieved some sort of mystical union. That this should be so is the mark of great poetry. Now, it is interesting to note that T.S. Eliot supposes Vaughan to be a 'minor religious poet' precisely because his poetry is the product of 'a special religious awareness, which may exist without the general awareness which we expect of the major poet'.[10] In other words, Vaughan's poetry is simply 'devotional poetry' – like say, Helen Steiner Rice. But this is surely not true! Some of his religious poetry is of this type no doubt, and Hutchison refers to certain of it as 'plodding couplets of conventional piety'. But most is far more universal in its appeal. Vaughan, of all people, is a generalist, not a specialist. He lived at a time when the particular symbols

---

[9] *Handel and his World.* Flamingo (Harper Collins), London, 1992, p. 285.

[10] 'Religion and Literature' in: *T.S. Eliot. Selected Essays.* Faber & Faber. 1972 (3rd ed).

and practices associated with his form of Anglicanism were shattered by the Civil War. As Kathleen Raine reminds us: 'Iconoclastic Protestantism largely destroyed, in England, the images which always had been, and must normally be, the natural language of spiritual knowledge'.[11] For this reason, if for no other, he was inclined to draw his inspiration from wider sources and, most especially, from the natural world around him.

Vaughan, in his treatment of the natural world, is often regarded as a precursor to the English Romantic Poets. This, I think, does not stand up to close scrutiny. Vaughan's nature was not Wordsworth's nature. It was at the same time a reflection of the Divine and a veil, obscuring the Divine. Vaughan, I think, would have agreed with William Blake – 'Mr Wordsworth must know that what he Writes Valuable is not to be found in Nature'. For all their praise of nature, the Romantics still tended to view it either as spectacle or, at best, as a sort of self-sufficient spiritual entity – in other words, a pantheistic view. Vaughan, on the other hand, takes a position more akin to certain of the early Church Fathers for whom the whole of nature shimmers with the reflection of the Divine. Augustine, for instance, writes of the spirit in this fashion: 'As the creative will of a sculptor hovers over a piece of wood, or as the spiritual soul spreads through all the limbs of the body; thus it is with the Holy Ghost; it hovers over all things with a creative and formative power'.[12] But there is an important distinction in Augustine's mind – because only God is good, perfect goodness is only to be found in

---

[11] *Defending Ancient Springs*. Oxford Univ. Press, 1985. p. 118.

[12] St. Augustine, *De genesi ad litteram*, IV, 16 (Quoted in Nasr, S.H. 1996. *Religion and the Order of Nature*. Oxford Univ. Press. p. 56.)

God. Nature participates in the good but is not the sole repository of the good. The order in nature issues from beyond nature. This is a key distinction and is one which Vaughan would have taken as self-evident.

One other point concerning Vaughan's view of nature is worth making. His poems are replete with examples of the whole of nature, right down to the very stones, praising God. Consider this short excerpt from "The Bird':

> ... All things that be, praise him; and had
> Their lesson taught them, when first made.
>
> So hills and valleys into singing break,
> And though poor stones have neither speech nor tongue,
> While active winds and streams both run and speak,
> Yet stones are deep in admiration.
> Thus praise and prayer beneath the sun
> Make lesser mornings, when the great are done.
>
> For each incloséd spirit is a star
> Enlightening his own little sphere,
> Whose light, though fetched and borrowed from far,
> Both mornings makes, and evenings there.

As Alan Rudrum points out, such a view was not common amongst the 'Metaphysicals'. Donne and Herbert, for instance, reject the idea.[13] Perhaps Vaughan had in mind those words from the Apocalypse of St John:

---

[13] Rudrum, op. cit., p. 606 (notes on the poems; '*The Bird*').

> And every creature which is in heaven, and on
> earth, and under the earth, and such as are in
> the sea, and all that are in them, heard I saying,
> Blessing, and honour, and glory, and power, be
> unto him that sitteth on the throne, and unto the
> Lamb for ever and ever. (5.13)

Whatever the case, it is abundantly clear that Vaughan's view of nature is a religious one, with deep affinities to Christian Platonism.

It is true that there are many enigmas in Vaughan's poetry, but I suspect these are of our making, not his. Vaughan can appear to hold the things of this earth in contempt, yet regard them as hierophantic. At some times, his poetry hints at an immanent spirituality, at others, a transcendent spirituality. His poetry can appear very simple yet, upon closer study, it reflects all of the complexities inherent in the Christian tradition. But it is the mark of a truly imaginative spirit that such contraries can be held together without conflict. Vaughan's best poetry transcends such concerns and draws upon a world of the imagination which is outside time and outside history. No one has put it better than Raine:

> Those who look to a timeless world are least likely
> to fall into archaisms of style, for the world of
> imagination is outside history altogether. Pope,
> Dryden and Auden are dated in a way that Dante,
> Milton, Coleridge, and Yeats, even when these
> embody in their imaginative world themes from
> history, can never be.[14]

I think I would be tempted to add to these two lists

---

[14] Ibid., p. 122.

given by Raine. To the first list of Pope, Dryden and Auden, I would add Eliot. To the second list, I would add Vaughan. *The Waste Land* may well reflect a modern, fragmented mind at the end of its tether, and it may well be the best poem of the last hundred years (as some think it is). But it can only have meaning in an age as terrible as ours. Vaughan's best poems, on the other hand, are outside the context of history and they supply an intellectual nourishment of real substance. They are, in all truth 'bright shoots of everlastingness'.

MAGAZINE SECTION

LANGUAGE, THOUGHT AND UNDERSTANDING

Clive Faust

Editor's Note: Previous selections from the aphorisms and aperçus of Clive Faust have been published in earlier issues of Connor Court Quarterly. *They exhibit an intellectual honesty now rare in academia and also display an acute awareness of and sensitivity to the limitations of the human condition.*

As La Rochefoucauld says, we assume that we will live forever – though we 'know' rationally that we won't. And there is a certain level of awareness, which seems physically situated in us, that is immortal, and is neither an aged man, a youth, a 'mature' adult, nor a child. No doubt it dies when we do, but it is easy to imagine it being unaffected even by that.

Not only does our body have a natural lifespan – if sometimes stopping a stage or two short of it – but our understanding has a natural lifespan too, managing two or three eras of cultural change in a lifetime, but giving up on any further adjustments to it after that.

I consistently see people, in unguarded moments, having insights, premonitions, empathies, discernments that they theoretically don't believe in. And their spiritual and mental poverty, starved by their unbelief, undernourishes them in time, just as physical poverty does. Not that they are to blame for that, and they've been educated to ignore such insights and accept their poverty as inevitable in the matter-of-fact and spiritless order of things.

The 'common understanding' has a regimen of quarantine, Customs and border security – 'to keep us all safe.'

How do you get certainty out of mere probability? You quantify probability into certainty – "at that degree of probability." And we know then, with some precision, how certain its probability is.

Breathtaking intellectual arrogance by people of monumental conformist stupidity is really the feature of the day. (It wasn't around like this when I was young – the 'acceptance' then was a different matter.) You are meant now to have exactly the insights that everyone else is supposed to have – and to imagine yourself as an 'individual' thinker for having them. They are bulk-manufacturing such Individual Thinkers.

I'm very resistant to "You know?" Normally "You know?" means "They know." And I'm not one of them. And I'm certainly not one of "us."

One predicts the probability of future events from past ones. But not only don't we have the evidence of future events themselves to predict from, we don't even have the future's understanding of what would then be considered relevant past events. So not only do we lack some data, we may also lack the method for assessing whatever data we have.

We've turned 'free' from a relational term – free from prison, free from pain – into an absolute – particularly as a noun with the "dom" at its back. It's one of our many words – like "individual" (not-divided) – that are basically negative, but that we strain to make positive, as if we needed something indisputably more substantial.

"Community values" instigated by media campaigns also have their use-by date. They become as unfashionable as commercial products advertised in another era – eventually becoming unsellable, then unprocurable.

With television you are rescued from time, and live outside life in a room without death. Through a window you see recurring events being repeated from many eras in a time that's always today, but never move on as today would. There are signs there are people outside the glass, but nobody moves in from outside to be with you.

A civilization can grow old, not having had anything but youthful experiences.

There really is a sense that psychology, even when it gets things wrong, is clearing the ground – or analysing the material – to reach a *complete* understanding of the human mind or character. Whereas what is happening is that we are reconstructing our understanding of the human to conform to psychological concepts, and even, that we begin to trim our behaviour, and certainly our self-analyses, to the concepts and explanations of this analytical set. So that, eventually, the explanations, the analyses actually do become closer to being true, as people's behaviour more and more closely conforms to them.

"What does 'life' mean to you? – assuming it means anything." If you're talking about the word "life", a dictionary definition would do it. If you're talking about LIFE ITSELF, I'm not sure why you've put the quotation marks in. But an answer: *words* have meaning; some signs have meaning in a derivative sense; but Life itself is neither meaningless nor meaningful. You can have a purpose in life, it's true, or two or three at different stages. And in this sense, life might have "meaning" for you. But Life itself has no meaning, nor does it lack one. Neither of these qualifiers is applicable to Life itself. To think of either of them as that is a category mistake – as if you could look up not just the words but Life Itself in a dictionary.

The dismissive phrases, "that's it," "when it comes down to it," "let's get down to the facts" – where the phrases have so much weight because they are brutalising reality, and one isn't allowed to nitpick about anything more complex that reality might be, but are bludgeoned into accepting "the obvious" that it is.

Disregard the judgments and opinions of the past? It's not that what's been said before is irrelevant, it's rather that what we took for *granted* had been said before is irrelevant.

"Religion is the opium of the people"? *Conformity* is the opium of the people, both in its religious and irreligious strains; and never more than when it has a deceptive air of older-style non-conformity about it to confuse everyone, including the alleged non-conformist himself.

For it is *today's* conformities that they will be hankering to conform to, however long or short a duration "today" is going to be.

Is life essentially dramatic? Or comic? Or do we have – as Bronk insists – no story, no history?

The barrister's job is to argue his client's case, not to seek for the truth, unless that suits his case. And he trains for the set of skills needed in debating tournaments and speech contests, where they nominate a subject of interest or of no interest to him – as the case may be – to argue for or against as directed.

In the process, he learns to transfer these skills and argue for himself as if he were a client, protecting whatever fortifications he happens to be standing in front of. It is similar in method to the salesman's task of promoting whatever goods he has in stock. The quality of the goods or of the stance is not an issue.

For the professional lawyer and salesman, these are their jobs – that's what they *ought* to be doing. But it would be intellectually perverted of us to forego the search for truth to find what specious arguments we might misshape for the purpose to buttress the position we happen to have, and not examine it to find its fault lines and cracks, and estimate whether the structure is still stable.

And the idea of winning or losing as the only alternatives, and that someone can receive a final decision on these matters in this courtroom – with no double-jeopardy on either side – must explicitly inhibit any journey over the lengths and breadths of the globe to see the vastness of the world's problems, and some hitherto undreamt-of possibilities for their solution.

"Many of our daily words are very vague and ambiguous." Like "very", "vague" and "ambiguous"? It depends on what standards you set up for them to fail to match. They give you vague thoughts very exactly. And "exactly" is not less vague, as a term, than "vague" is – or, really, "vague" is as exact a term as "exactly."

Rationalism itself is not something deduced rationally, but a leap of unfaith into a world stripped bare of resonance, and articulated into separate things with space between them, and no haze confusing you as to where and what things are. It's an approach to life very common everywhere, in use for practical matters, where the aims are clear and known in advance; but was never before intended to be the only understanding of things, nor used negatively as a test for all other approaches that have ever been made; and is not reinforced by the dictum – itself without evidence – that no other approach would be possible.

Like other beliefs, it has a vision – a world in which there is no uncertainty – about things in the world or ideas in the mind. Fogs – both physical and mental – are to be isolated, so that nothing else is finally obscured by them.

And a divine clarity, and clear space, is the medium that will enable you to keep all objects distinct, even the fogs.

The logical basis for this vision would be the Aristotelian Laws of Identity – where each thing is what it is, is not what it's not, and there is no third alternative, an Excluded Middle, between the two. These Laws have a few logical problems themselves – as the one about Relationships, or the one about Category Mistakes; but Rationalism is a belief system, and any inroads like this into it are treated like cul-de-sacs, or the worst of sophist saboteurs. And the whole world is to be converted, and the feeble enemy subdued, so that the clear light of truth may pervade this universe, and be unencumbered by both the clouds of dust and the boggy marshes of superstition that these ancient marauders and their priests attempted to clog up the clarity with. It's an attractive vision of what the world could be like, but the difficulty they have convincing everyone of its viability hints, at the very least, that it's not obviously what the world is like; and they have never suggested any transition method for proceeding from what the world is now to this new world they are advocating, where all the problems of the old one will become obsolete.

"What is the meaning of a flower? What is the meaning of anything?" Things don't mean anything, and they don't mean nothing either. *Words* mean something (or some do), and things can be granted a meaning at a remove. *Then*, they don't mean nothing, because they've been granted/ bestowed/dubbed a meaning: "Arise Sir Thingaling!"

With medicine, a lot of the terms are just Latin or Greek equivalents of the English words they've ousted:

"patella" just means "kneecap" and more importantly, "uterus" just means "womb" (in Latin). There's no new scientific discovery comes with this jargon, and the words shouldn't have been replaced. They were, just so educated (Latin) people ("doctors" to use another Latin word) could get purchase on it from Latin, the once universal language of education, and keep the knowledge in house. Not that most "doctors" know it now, so that for them it is as dead a language as it is for us.

I know, I was talking to a medico about stress fractures of the foot, and he used the term "navicular bone." I suggested it might come from "navis" a ship – and it was a (capsized) boat shape. So there wasn't even that much resonance for him.[1] But even if we know these terms, we learn them as without resonance. We learn them as "precise", "distinctive". O.K. with kneecap turning into "patella" perhaps. But what about "uterus" usurping "womb"? All sorts of experience trashed with the term, in favour of one from a dead language that no longer has *its* resonance with it.

If I were to "purify the language of the tribe", that sort of reconnection with experience – if it could be done – would be the way I'd do it. Meanwhile, I'd like to rescue any older words I could (esp. in important areas) – older English words, that is, if only for nostalgia.

"To face whatever it is." I have some sympathy for this objective. But it is by no means clear what is; and if it seems to be clear, that is not because it has been discovered, but because it has been presupposed.

[1] Not my own regular doctor, by the way, who's quite savvy.

When a friend dies it often breaks a longstanding argument you're having with him, sometimes about matters of importance. The points you want to score have no target any more, while his points hang in the air and have suddenly become unanswerable – as it's impolite, as well as impossible, to argue with the dead.

One of the joys with kids is to see them vibrantly snapping up our platitudes of understanding as their own discoveries, their minds opening out to a world of new truths – ones we can be very comfortable with. It's called "Educating the Young". Later, in adolescence, they see the deficiencies in such platitudes, and make us quite uncomfortable with their barbs. For they have moved with the times, and can now understand such platitudes – though not yet their own – to be as deficient as they always were.

One of the commonplace assumptions is that solid ordinary people don't philosophize, but only intellectual wankers spouting airy-fairy nonsense. On the back of this assumption, the commonplace philosophical positions are seen as "obvious", "realistic" and the rest – not as positions at all. It should cause queries, when such positions change; but the later arrivals into the commonplace just see (as always) the contemporary positions as being "obvious", while the older positions are something we've grown out of – if they're different. Following such conventional thought patterns, most people, without knowing it, do quite a bit of philosophizing, and even (sometimes quite bad) logic. So there is a place for logical correctives in "real life" – which is often a lot more airy-fairy than that phrase would normally have us believe.

All our thinking words (excepting "think" itself) and most of our feeling ones are metaphorical – "see", "understand", "enlighten", "track it down", "feeling" itself, "distinguish", "separate" (as in space), "conclusion", "elucidate", "it breaks my heart", "I'm stunned by it", "well-grounded". The Latinate ones don't look it, and not just because we can't construe Latin, but because people want to "look at things objectively", and don't want to think of their methods and categories of understanding as having a metaphorical base. And the Latinate words can seem so much more objective because their metaphorical base is in an unknown dead language. Though even in a living language the metaphor will go dead – as in "understand" (stand under), or in "base" itself.

I wonder if you can't undercut Occam's Razor – showing that the category of Unnecessary Metaphysical Entities is itself an unnecessary metaphysical entity? The unkindest undercut of all?

Probably not – as it's a negative not a positive – and so not an entity as such, but a useful rule of avoidance, to cut our metaphysical costs.

The idea of "God" is a mobile concept. It shifts from immanent to transcendent and back again, confusing the issue and dodging theological bullets – and accusations of heresy backed by torture at the stake. While the confusion thus created is meant to be a "mystery of religion" – that you are meant to get very genuflective about – rather than theological stuff-up. In its wake, certain doctrinal necessities – like the Three Persons of the Trinity – truncated into one domineering overlord that you are meant, cringingly to love – become devotionally inoperative.

We "reasonablists" have the feeling that the past was dark and evil – except at the fringes, where the truth was painfully being born. Evil usually because of some particular viciousness – violence, patriarchy, repression (including psychological) or superstition. And that it would all hang around like a foul smell, or at best a musty odour, before it was blown away by the fresh winds of today.

The most important thing you learn in the academy is why it's not to be overestimated. It's something you need to learn, for all that. There are some modest virtues in scholarship, and the popular view of it ("wankers") is inadequate. Their own view of themselves, however, is as overinflated as the paper bag they are forever about to pop.

The powers-that-be are certainly aware of this particular psycho-sociologic, and have encouraged rebellious styles in fashion, in music, clothes and attitudes, to divert any latent rebellion into frivolous pursuits. In fact, they have corralled both the rebellion and the reaction to it into a self-contained ricochetting dialectic, which can't escape out into the free world of ideas, where that reality might have disrupted the dialect's internal patterning and re-patterning.

Abstractions usually have their time spans attached to them – think of the 18th century's "sublime". The ostensibly more enduring ones, like "essence", have more than once changed their meanings without notice, usually dragging the echoes of the earlier meanings along in their wake. They can also change into their opposites – so that "essence" and "substance" become interchangeable.

Yes, we *can* shift "community opinion" by blurring the boundaries, so that, for example patting bottoms becomes a form of rape. And for a while "rape" will still mean rape, too. After that, though, the fudging of boundaries will be complete, and rape itself will seem very much more like the patting of bottoms than it could ever have seemed before – so the edge in the public's mind would have been blunted. This is the advertiser's trick – and the Community Advertiser's trick – to gain a competitive edge. But it only lasts for a time, and after the boundaries have been finally blurred, the language will have been contaminated permanently and – apart from anything else – will no longer again be manipulable for this particular sophistry.

"Things are getting worse." "Oh, but that's what people have always said." "Why shouldn't this be evidence that it's true? I bet if people had always said, 'things are getting better', it would be taken as evidence that that particular proposition was true."

****

Clive Faust has been many things, public service clerk, professional gambler, school teacher, and reluctant academic, both in Japan and Australia. By preference, he is a poet. For many years he contributed to Origin magazine (U.S.), edited by the late Cid Corman. Five collections of his poetry have been published in the U.S., Australia and New Zealand.

BOOK REVIEW

Boschiero, L. (Ed). *On The Purpose of a University Education.* Aust. Scholarly Publishing, Melbourne, 2013.

Reviewed by Roger Sworder

This is an exceptionally good book on its subject, and it is the record of a signal occasion. Four of the papers here were delivered at a workshop at Campion College, Sydney, on one day in December 2011. They were the only papers delivered that day and they are all unusually valuable. Certainly, they all address their subject from points of view I value highly. The fifth paper, by Arran Gare, is quite as valuable and a crucial addition. The editor also provides an introduction.

The five essays draw on a very wide range of sources. Our current problems are seen against a large backdrop of earlier and contemporary understandings. Constant Mews opens by examining the jockeying between grammar and logic in the disputes between Hugh of St. Victor and Abelard. Mews sets himself the difficult task of showing the plasticity of the liberal arts in the twelfth century, how the organising of them in accordance with the latest theories and discoveries generated many different schemes. It was a ferment, much less structured than I had imagined, a contest between grammar and logic to be the handmaid of theology. Mews fixes our attention on the parallel between that ferment and our own. Similarly, though over a much longer period, Arran Gare explores earlier debates about the nature and order of the liberal arts from the Renaissance until now. He is particularly strong on the German Idealist philosophers around the turn of the nineteenth century and locates his own intellectual centre in the work of Schelling. What a relief it always is to turn from the aridity of the British Empiricists to the Olympian intellectual aspirations of the Germans! I have the liveliest suspicion that the German philosophy of the time expressed exactly those impulses which we find also in the great Classical and Romantic symphonies. As Gare shows, the theory of the Humboldtian university is critical to our present concerns.

In the last essay, Gregory Melleuish traces the line from the Cambridge Platonists to Matthew Arnold's conception of culture, emphasising what we have learnt to call the *praxis* of the inward or spiritual life as opposed to debating it. This has much in common with the German notion of *bildung*, as it is explained by Arran Gare. Melleuish gives an extended account of the seventeenth century Platonists and quotes movingly from them and from those who followed them.

But these powerful recreations of the liberal arts in earlier incarnations are only part of that large backdrop which this book brings into focus. It is quite as strong in its account of the contemporary. Here I must confess to a particular liking for Stephen McInerney's essay *Integration* which examines the arguments for and against constructing Arts courses across several majors as opposed to the smorgasbord approach now nearly universal. We ran an integrated program of this kind in Bendigo for over twenty years. Warmly appreciated by its undergraduates, it was also a very effective foundation for postgraduate work in a very large number of different fields in the

Arts. McInerney brings to bear a much wider range of contemporary scholarship on these issues than I had studied, and I am very grateful. Studying the same periods in different disciplines in more or less chronological order allows the student to appreciate each new period from the perspective of that period itself and its inheritance. What could be more straightforward or more effective? Our Bendigo program even had the same obvious name as the one in Campion College, except that we called it Studies in Western Traditions (in the plural).

As for the smorgasbord approach, it is much more pliant to the pressures of Academic administration and it can always be justified as *empowering* the student by granting the student freedom of choice. But students do not come to University to seek freedom of choice once they have chosen what they wish to do. That choice made, they want the most competent teaching and direction they can find. As for Arts teachers who prefer a wide range of choices within programs, they seem to me to manifest a reluctance to take responsibility for the direction of students within their fields.

Another essay in this book gives an account of the liberal arts in the University of Sydney from its founding until now. Geoffrey Sherington and Hannah Forsyth illuminate the influence first of the Empire and then of the OECD on the formulation of the policy settings of the university, as well as the strong commitment of many vice-chancellors and professors to an elite general education for disinterested mandarins. They trace in detail the slow emergence of the university as a means simply to the maintenance and advancement of a technocratic society whose goals are beyond discussion. This itself is a huge shift from the university as an independent and autonomous institution with its own goals, which the rest of the social order should serve as needed. It is even further from the Medieval notion that the university helped in some cases to produce that highest of all social achievements, the saint.

I went to university for free in England and at the farewell dinner for undergraduates in my program and College, my tutor expressed the view that free university tuition was a mistake. Nor was he dissuaded from this view when I told him that I could not have attended otherwise. In the beginning, he said, universities were autonomous, charged fees and awarded scholarships. Then the government said that it would pay the fees but the universities would reman autonomous. Next the government will say that since it is paying the fees it deserves some say in the running of the universities. Then the government will say that the country has fallen on hard times and it can no longer afford to pay the fees. But strangely there will be no returning of autonomy to the universities. And he was right.

All this is not surprising. The subordination of ancient and autonomous institutions to the authority of the State is characteristic of English history, especially spiritual institutions. At least in this transformation the Arts have all the other faculties to commiserate with. So I am, I think, less shocked by what is happening to the Arts now than Melleuish or Gare or the editor, Luciano Boschiero. The loss of the ideal of learning for its own sake or strictly as a means to spiritual development seems to me to have happened long ago. Each step of the downward staircase should indeed be furiously resisted, but it is a much longer staircase than it looks and we are much further down it.

And there is another consideration which again applies to all the faculties. It will not, it seems, be the internal demands of commercial or bureaucratic utility which are most destructive of university eduction. All that was done long ago. Now through electronics the acts of lecturing and tutoring are themselves under serious threat. What has happened to making music is happening to teaching: its usurpation by the recording industry. With a little research the businessmen have found a way of putting our wages too in their pockets. What percentage of the lecturing workforce will disappear? This robotisation must lead finally to a kind of magic toyshop as marvellous for its effects as for the underdevelopment of its customers.

jgd graphic+web

www.jgd.com.au

LETTER TO THE EDITOR

Dear Editor,

I would like to comment concerning the article "William Blake and the Perversion of Pity" (*Connor Court Quarterly, No. 4*). With the Industrial Revolution and the enclosure movement, the British population began to increase rapidly for very simple reasons: people were no longer starving to death, more children were surviving infancy, more mothers were surviving child-birth, and people were generally living longer than had been the case in pre-industrial times. The population of England and Wales in 1700 had been about 5,500,000 (not much different to what it had been for centuries). By 1750, in the earliest part of the Agrarian and Industrial Revolutions, it had reached 6,500,000 – a huge increase. When the first census was taken in 1801, the population was 9,000,000 and by 1830 it had reached 14,000,000.

It is a false myth, concocted by the political Left, and propagated by those who have never read his work, that Adam Smith believed in laissez-faire. Smith believed in minimal regulation. He supported State-funded education to enable the poor to better themselves, and recommended that they be given opportunities to change their employment to promote upward social mobility, and also to allow them to escape mental and moral stultification, or, as he put it, "the vilest and most abject" of all states, insensibility to vice and virtue (Theory of Moral Sentiments, various editions). As a propagandist against industrialisation,

William Blake was a propagandist for poverty and death. Smith was a propagandist for life.

Hal G. P. Colebatch

Dorothy Avery Replies:

I thank Dr Colebatch for his vigorous and pertinent reply to my article. There does indeed seem to have been a decline in the death rate in the later 18th century. There was certainly the beginning of a population explosion that was to go on for more than another 150 years. We may speculate on the reasons for this too, but among them we would need to consider the effects of massive social and cultural dislocation, tremendous urban compression, and sheer human misery.

For every historian who claims that the Agrarian and Industrial Revolutions were of immense benefit to the under classes of Britain there are as many who decry them. It is possible to throw historians at each other, but unhelpful.

Blake was a member of the working-poor class, with a roof over his head, some food on the table and the support of good friends and admirers. But he grieved for those who were not as fortunate as he.

> Can I see another's woe,
>
> And not be in sorrow too?

The plight of the children at that time moved Blake to write some of his most beautiful and moving poems. In 1789 he published 'Songs of Innocence', which contains 23 poems. Eleven of these are about the plight of children, including the chimney sweep.[1] To call Blake 'a propagandist for poverty and death' is to take far too long a view of a present and pressing human misery. Blake saw in every human being the potential offered by Christ's sacrifice. This was not recognised by those who mistreated men, women or children and mistreatment or plain neglect was the norm.

When Gandhi was asked what he thought of Western civilisation, he replied that it would be a good idea. Whatever else, his reply is surely not incomprehensible. And it is a very striking fact how often the poets abhor the new order. Not only Eliot and Pound, but E. A. Robinson, Melville, Kipling, Chesterton, Morris, Yeats. The following is by Yeats.

> Locke sank into a swoon;
> The Garden died;
> God took the spinning-jenny
> Out of his side.

The resistance to the new science goes all the way back to Pope's 'Dunciad'. So were Gandhi and all these poets just sentimentalists, as Karl Marx would have us believe? Propagandists for poverty and death?

D. J. Avery

---

[1] Trevelyan attributes the success of Charles Kingsley's *Water Babies* to the passing of the Chimney-Sweeper's Act of 1864. William Blake was writing about the life of the sweeps in 1789 and, again, in 1789-1794 in 'Songs of Experience', 22 poems in all, of which 8 are about children.

103

CHRISTIANITY AND
THE LIBERAL ARTS

If you are interested in reviving the values associated with the liberal arts, *Connor Court Quarterly* Issue 5/6 is required reading. Some of the more important essays include:

Cardinal Newman and the Modern University
 Steven Schwartz
The Sad Universities That We Have Become
 Paul Collits
Walter Scott and Catholic Truth?
 Michael Alexander
James McAuley and the End of Modernity
 Greg Melleuish
Latin, the Bearer of our Heritage
 Richard Conolly
Michael Oakeshott on the Character of University
 Education *Ian Tregenza*
Christopher Dawson and the Intelligibility
 of the Integrative Cultural Process
 James Gaston
Reinventing the Liberal Arts
 Wayne Hudson
Modern Intellectual Misery and Chesterton's Creed
 of Limits *Peter Murphy*
The Catholic Histories of Warren Carroll and Eamon
 Duffy *Philippa Martyr*
T.S. Eliot and the Western Classical Tradition
 Barry Spurr

History, Theology and Development in the Thought
of Newman *Stephen McInerney*

Available now from Connor Court Publishing:

www.connorcourt.com

Price: $29.95

www.ingramcontent.com/pod-product-compliance
Lightning Source LLC
Chambersburg PA
CBHW060547100426
42742CB00013B/2487